RESTRICTIVE BUSINESS PRACTICES, TRANSNATIONAL CORPORATIONS, AND DEVELOPMENT

DIMENSIONS OF
INTERNATIONAL BUSINESS

Restrictive Business Practices, Transnational Corporations, and Development
A Survey

Frank Long

Queen Elizabeth House, Oxford

Martinus Nijhoff Publishing

Boston/The Hague/London

DISTRIBUTORS FOR NORTH AMERICA:
Martinus Nijhoff Publishing
Kluwer Boston, Inc.
190 Old Derby Street
Hingham, Massachusetts 02043, U.S.A.

DISTRIBUTORS OUTSIDE NORTH AMERICA:
Kluwer Academic Publishers Group
Distribution Centre
P.O. Box 322
3300 AH Dordrecht, The Netherlands

Library of Congress Cataloging in Publication Data

Long, Frank.
  Restrictive business practices, transnational
corporations, and development.

  (Dimensions of international business; 2)
  Includes index.
  1. International business enterprises. 2. Restraint
of trade. 3. Industrial concentration. 4. Underdeveloped areas—International business enterprises.
5. Economic development. I Title. II. Series.
HD2755.5.L66   338.8′8   80–24652

ISBN 0-89838-057-X

To Zemenay

CONTENTS

Acknowledgments   xi

Introduction   xiii

1   THE PROBLEM   1
    Definition of Terms   1
    The Concepts of Oligopoly and Monopoly and Restrictive
      Business Practices   2
    Business Concentration and the Real World   12
    Market Power and the Law   17

2   LITERATURE ON DEVELOPMENT   18
    Growth and Development   18
    The 1950s to the Early 1960s   19
    International Aspects   24
    Toward a Social Scientific Interpretation   28
    Conclusion   29

3 RESTRICTIVE BUSINESS PRACTICES, TRANSNATIONAL
CORPORATIONS, AND ASPECTS OF CONTROL   30
    Legislation in Selected Developed Countries   30
    Legislation in Developing Countries   41

4 TRANSNATIONAL CORPORATIONS AND
DEVELOPING COUNTRIES   47
    Investment Theory, International Investment,
      and Transnationals   50
    Transnational Corporations as Dominant-Firm Types 52
    Activities of Transnational Corporations and
      Developing Countries   57
    Country Breakdown of Production Activities   62
    Transnational Corporations and Imports   65
    Transnational Corporations and Exports   70

5 RESTRICTIVE BUSINESS PRACTICES AND
TRANSNATIONAL CORPORATIONS: SOME AVAILABLE
EVIDENCE   75
    Types of Restrictive Business Practices   75
    Restrictive Business Practices and Transnational
      Corporations: The Factual Situation   81

6 DEVELOPMENT IMPLICATIONS OF RESTRICTIVE
BUSINESS PRACTICES   101
    Some Negative Aspects   102
    Imports   111
    Exports   115
    A Summary of Development Implications   116
    Other Related Aspects   118
    Conclusion   122

7 POLICY ASPECTS OF RESTRICTIVE
BUSINESS PRACTICES   123
    Historical Aspects   123
    UNCTAD and Restrictive Business Practices   124
    Other Cases   129

Conclusions   135

Notes   137

Name Index   159

Subject Index   161

ACKNOWLEDGMENTS

This study has benefited from the comments of Professor Peter Bernholz at the Institüt für Sozialwissenschaften, Basel, and an unnamed referee from the Massachusetts Institute of Technology. It is the outcome of work on transnational corporations and restrictive business practices that began at the Secretariat of the United Nations Conference on Trade and Development in Geneva, in 1975. Preparation of the study was done at the Institüt für Sozialwissenschaften and, for the greater part, at Queen Elizabeth House, Oxford. The author alone bears the final responsibility for whatever shortcomings are found in the study.

INTRODUCTION

Problems of development in what is normally called the Third World have been a subject matter of concern of the social sciences, especially of economics, for over two decades now.[1] Between the late 1950s and the current time, as Chapter 2 attempts to show, the emphasis seems to have shifted from purely economic considerations of underdevelopment to a paradigm that includes other, extra-economic considerations of a social, political, and cultural nature. The recent emergence of development studies as a new social science discipline stems precisely from the methodological premise that development is a complex process that can only be adequately understood, analyzed, and alleviated by a cross-disciplinary approach instead of a wholly unidisciplinary one.[2]

We do not wish to challenge the above proposition. However, it remains true that an assessment of certain economic phenomena that pose problems to developing countries can offer us greater insights into problems of development, including the formulation of appropriate policies aimed at improving socioeconomic conditions in such countries.

One such phenomenon is restrictive business practices. This study is concerned mainly with surveying aspects of restrictive business practices as they relate to problems of development in the Third World. Restrictive business practices are not confined to developing countries; however, limited work seems to have been conducted in terms of relating the concept of restrictive business practices to problems of development. The existing evidence of restrictive business practices in the development process is quite fragmentary.

This study is not concerned with restrictive business practices in a general sense. We are specifically concerned with restrictive business practices that involve transnational corporations.[3] Restrictive business practices may involve national firms as well, but these do not concern us in this study.

We justify the emphasis of this study on the following grounds:

- No systematic attempt exists in terms of relating restrictive business practices of transnational corporations to problems of development in the Third World; this remains so in spite of increasing interest in transnational corporations.
- Transnational corporations are an important feature in the economic life of most economies of the Third World—through production, trade, or both.
- Transnational corporations, as we will show, generally operate under market conditions that potentially give rise to forms of restrictive business practices.

The survey attempts to show the following:

- Restrictive business practices involving transnational corporations appear widespread insofar as they relate to economies of the Third World.
- Such practices tend to hamper the development process of many Third World economies.
- As a result, restrictive business practices involving transnational corporations can be considered important in the study of underdevelopment.

The outline of this study is as follows: Chapter 1 deals with definition of terms, the concepts of oligopoly and monopoly and their relevance to the study of restrictive business practices, dynamic aspects of competition, market concentration and the real world, and market power and the law. Chapter 2 is concerned with surveying the literature on development for the purpose of illustrating the analytical neglect of restrictive business practices legislation in selected countries. The chapter attempts to show that most legislation fails to include adequate controls over transnational corporations and their activities as these affect developing countries. Chapter 3 examines aspects of control. Chapter 4 looks at the activities of transnational corporations in developing countries. The argument here is that a large number of important transnational corporations tend to operate in grossly imperfect markets. Further, Chapter 4 attempts to show the importance of transnational corporations in the economies of developing countries. Chapter 5 examines the available evidence of restrictive business practices of transnational corporations in developing countries. Chapter 6 represents an attempt to discuss some of the problems of restrictive business practices and development. Chapter 7 looks at some policy aspects of the problem. The book ends with a brief conclusion that summarizes the entire study and indicates its implications for future research.

1 THE PROBLEM

This chapter looks at the general problem of restrictive business practices. It focuses on the definition of terms, the concepts of oligopoly and monopoly and restrictive business practices, business concentration and the real world, and market power and the law.

DEFINITION OF TERMS

Restrictive business practices are variously defined. Most of the definitions concern the questions of market dominance by one firm and collusiveness involving two or more firms, and their consequences for competition.[1] The concept therefore relates to market asymmetry and is relevant to the study of imperfect rather than perfect markets. In this study, restrictive business practices are regarded as attempts by firms to "restrain competition, limit access to markets, or foster monopolistic control."[2] The concept is essentially a legal one, although its explanation is to be found in the behavior of firms. As Chapter 3 shows, restrictive business practices are regulated under the national laws of many countries. Clearly, this would seem to necessitate strategic considerations by firms—hence, the relevance of collusiveness and other types of behavior, such as those relating to pricing, output, and marketing. Evidence suggests that a collusive strategy frequently involves one or more of the following considerations: aspects of price fixing, product-sharing arrangements, control over promotion and distribution channels, market allocation arrangements, mergers and takeovers, and other attempts at market control. These aspects of collusive behavior are prominent in most legal complaints involving the use of restrictive business practices. They are, for example, well documented in various official reports on competition policy in Europe and North America.[3]

An exception to the rule of collusiveness would exist, in principle, where there is only one firm dominating an industry. An extreme case in point is the pure monopolist. In such a case, it makes little sense to adopt a collusive strategy with another firm or firms. The dominant firm is able to "restrain competition, limit access to markets, or foster (greater) monopolistic control" on its own, so that it can continue to reap abnormal profits. One way of doing so would be by discriminatory pricing. There are surely others. Under perfect competition, for example, free market entry will persist, and higher product prices will tend to induce potential firms to enter the market in order to maximize profits. In the final equilibrium state, abnormal profits will cease to exist, with competitive forces resulting in a corresponding increase in supply, which brings about a reduction of prices.

Thus, market domination, which is often regarded as synonymous with market control, has come to be regarded as "the position occupied either by a single enterprise or by a group of enterprises between which no effective competition exists."[4]

THE CONCEPTS OF OLIGOPOLY AND MONOPOLY
AND RESTRICTIVE BUSINESS PRACTICES

It follows that the theory of the firm is a useful starting point for the study of restrictive business practices. Firms operate in different markets. The type of market relevant here, however, is, as we just saw, the imperfect market. The normal assumptions of perfect competition, such as an unlimited number of buyers and sellers, perfect information, perfect factor mobility, freedom of market entry, parametric market prices, and product homogeneity, mean that individual firms are unable to influence market prices and conduct. A firm or group of firms likewise is unable to adopt a strategy for market control since the assumptions preclude forms of market control. This Marshallian notion of the firm has not been without criticism, as evidenced by Sraffa's criticism in the 1920s and Chamberlain's and Robinson's in 1933. Essentially, their argument was that the real market situation was characterized by forms of market imperfection. Sraffa argued, for instance, that "it is necessary to abandon the path of free competition and turn in the opposite direction, namely towards monopoly."[5] Robinson contended that perfect competition was, in fact, "a special case" rather than the typical one.[6] And Chamberlain's position was that "both monopolistic and competitive forces combine in the determination of most prices, and therefore a hybrid theory affords a more illuminating approach to the study of the price system than does a theory of perfect competition supplemented by a theory of monopoly."[7]

The study of firms in imperfect markets can be classified broadly as follows: monopolistic competition, oligopoly, and monopoly. In a nutshell, the Chamberlain model of monopolistic competition differs from perfect competition in that the typical firm produces differentiated products instead of homogeneous ones. Substitutes are therefore imperfect, the implication being that some element of "monopoly" is associated with the differentiated product. The demand curve facing the firm is therefore downward-sloping instead of horizontal. Provision is also made for selling expenditure. However, the presence of a large group of firms in the industry and free market access by new firms operate to ensure competitiveness. In other words, each firm produces a small part of the market output, but it has some overall influence on prices. Because of product differentiation, the firm is also unable to determine the rules of the market game. Competitiveness here ensures that in the final equilibrium state, abnormal profits are ruled out. In this state, marginal costs are equal to marginal revenue, but average revenue or price is higher than both of these, given the downward-sloping nature of the firm's demand curve already mentioned.[8] The Robinson model is essentially similar.

The above paradigm is not strictly relevant for our purposes, despite its usefulness in other respects. What is needed is a concept of gross market imperfection, such as oligopoly or monopoly. Most forms of restrictive business practices legislation, for example, regard a significant share of the market by a single firm to be consistent with market dominance or statutory monopoly. This, of course, varies—in the United Kingdom, it is 25 percent; in the United States, it is 90 percent. In France, "manifest concentration of economic power" is the criterion, while in the Federal Republic of Germany, market domination is defined in terms of "absence of substantial competition."[9] Surely, then, the Robinson-Chamberlain firm type fails to satisfy this criterion. Often, the collusive practices referred to in the preceding section involve firms that, as a group, are able to command a large share of the market so that jointly they can influence prices, profits, and conditions of market entry.

Most textbook models of the firm operating in imperfect markets do not discuss restrictive business practices in any comprehensive sense. However, some of the models can be extended to incorporate this consideration more seriously.

The case of pure monopoly is well treated in cconomic theory, and we do well by starting here. Strictly speaking, the pure monopolist is the sole producer of a product. The firm is not only a firm but also the industry. Product competition is nonexistent. The "pure monopolist" has complete market power and is able to take the whole of all consumers' incomes at whatever level the firm's output is set.[10]

The case of the pure monopolist is quite unrealistic on a number of counts. For example, products compete with each other for limited consumers' income, and so there is in fact a limit to a firm's power to fix prices. Also, for our present purpose, the pure monopolist does not represent the real-world case of market dominance, even though it does pose, in principle, some of the price and output problems one tends to encounter in situations of market dominance.

More practical models of monopoly deal with cases in which a firm controls the supply of a particular product for which there are no close substitutes (although substitutes do exist) or a large share of the market for a particular product, as in the case of statutory monopolies referred to earlier. The profit-maximizing monopolist here can be operating under conditions in which marginal costs are rising, falling, or constant. In competitive situations, they are rising. The point to bear in mind is that whether pure monopolist or not, the profit-maximizing monopolist will tend to earn abnormal profits in the long run—he is able to charge high prices for his products given the absence of close substitutes, and therefore of competition, and produces to the point where his marginal costs are equal to marginal revenue. The degree of monopoly profits depends on the shape of the average revenue or demand curve. The more inelastic the curve, the greater the scope for monopoly profits.

In principle, two types of restrictive business practices can be identified in the above situation. One is that the monopolist is able to restrict output in an effort to earn high monopoly profits. Also, he is able to engage in discrimination in different markets characterized by varying price elasticities of demand, with respect to either prices or output, and is therefore able not only to maximize profits but also to keep out potential competitors. For example, by charging arbitrarily low prices, sometimes referred to as limit pricing, he is able to keep out competitors in an effort to maximize long-run profits.

Given his market power, the monopolist is not necessarily forced by competitive pressures to produce at the lowest point possible along the firm's cost curve. If, however, one assumes for the sake of argument that costs of production are indeed the lowest possible, the monopolist is still able to charge relatively high product prices to consumers. In other words, low-cost output does not necessarily benefit consumers in the form of low product prices.

The assumption that the monopolist is not operating at the lowest point on the average revenue curve means that the critique against the monopolist—namely, resource misallocation—holds. Further, high monopoly profits will tend to introduce distortions in the factor markets and therefore in the functional distribution of income. The reduction of income inequality is often regarded as a social objective in the preference function of most governments. Under assumptions of an open economy, other consequences can follow—for example, lack of international competitiveness and therefore reduced welfare for a particular economy.[11]

The problem with monopoly models, however, is that while the marketplace of modern industrial societies tends to be characterized by big business, such business is not the type one finds in monopoly theory. Rather, it tends to be of an oligopolistic nature—that is, a number of large firms coexist in a market rather than there being just one single firm. In theory, however, it is possible for a group of large firms to constitute the textbook type of monopolist simply by adopting "collusive market strategies" so that, functionally, the effect in terms of pricing and output that can be obtained is the same as if the group were a single firm. Still, the situation is not strictly analogous, as a prisoner's dilemma can develop in a collusive arrangement whereby the whole "deal," or part of it, collapses. Alternatively, one may opt for a diluted concept of monopoly, such as the one found in legislation—namely, market-dominating enterprises—where, as we saw, a sizable share of the market is the main criterion. But it should be noted that in this case, some competition would exist in the product market since there are also competing firms, albeit large ones. Even so, the dominant firm is able to exert some control over the market, in terms of prices and output, though to a lesser extent than if it had complete control of the market. In this situation, the dominant firm may be operating in an oligopolistic market. The concept of oligopoly brings us closer to home.

The basic oligopoly/duopoly model used in economics was first developed by Cournot.[12] Essentially, the Cournot model results in determinate solutions for price and output, usually under very strict assumptions. For example, one central assumption is that Firm 1 would conjecture about how its rival, Firm 2, would vary output in response to Firm 1's market decisions. This conjectural variation in Cournot's model is zero. In other words, Firm 1 decides what level of output to produce on the assumption that the rival firm would not vary output in response to this.[13] If data are available on costs and on the average revenue curves of each firm, it is possible to derive Firm 2's profit-maximizing responses to any output set by Firm 1, assuming a conjectural variation of zero for Firm 2—in other words, Firm 2's reaction function. Given this response symmetry, it is also possible to obtain Firm 1's profit-maximizing or reaction function. This is shown in Figure 1.1. Firm 1 initially produces output y, Firm 2's reaction function results in output x, Firm 1 opts for output y_2 (its own reaction function), and Firm 2 responds to x_2. The process continues until equilibrium is reached at point A, where both reaction functions intersect.

The Cournot model is in many respects an uninteresting one for the analysis of restrictive business practices. In particular, it assumes a state of "independence" in the sense that Firm 1's actions do not influence Firm 2's output decisions. This does not seem quite realistic. As Chamberlain argues, interdependence rather than independence is a feature of oligopolistic behavior. Thus, according to Chamberlain, "If each sees his maximum

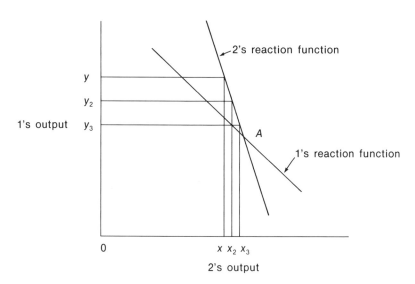

FIGURE 1.1.   Oligopolistic Reaction: An Illustration

profit position rationally and intelligently, he will realize that when there are only two or a few sellers his own move has considerable effect upon his competitors and that it makes it idle to suppose that they will accept without retaliation the losses he forces upon them."[14] According to the Chamberlain position, it is possible for a joint profit-maximizing price to be reached in these circumstances. Once this price has been attained, a firm will be unable to reduce price since it will assume that others will respond and profits will be adversely affected, and price competition will thereby be eliminated. In effect, although sellers are legally distinct, the equilibrium situation will be as if "there were a monopolistic agreement between them," in the manner mentioned earlier. In other words, this amounts to a form of collusive pricing behavior found in many empirical investigations of monopoly type of market practices. Such behavior can be open or tacit.

However, Chamberlain's position regarding joint profit-maximization prices will apply only where all firms have identical costs and revenue properties. It is possible, for instance, for technological and learning-by-doing economies to result in different cost profiles among firms. Also, different demand curves might be the result of product differentiation, sales promotion, and the like. In this case, different firms will want different profit-maximizing prices. Nevertheless, in the interest of long-run stability, agreements concerning market behavior are, in principle, possible. For example, markets could be allocated to different producers so that prices reflect individual producer's cost and demand considerations. Brand-name pooling is also possible so that more established firms "compensate" less established firms in terms of having assured market outlets for their products. In this way, high profits are assured for less established firms. In like manner, joint promotional efforts could be made that discriminate positively in favor of less established firms, again following a welfare compensation principle. The agreements here will take a different form from the pure-pricing type suggested by Chamberlain. In either case, competition will tend to be restricted first among the "given group" of agreeing firms and second against outsiders. In the latter case, different entry-forestalling strategies that keep out potential entrants are possible—for instance, predatory pricing or freezing distributional channels.[15] However, as Stigler has shown, problems arise in enforcing agreements of the type just described.[16]

Another development in oligopoly behavior refers to von Stackelberg's leader-follower model.[17] Here, the dominant firm A assumes a leadership role, meaning that other firms treat A's output or price as given and proceed to establish their market conduct on that basis. In this case, a determinate stable equilibrium is reached. If two leading firms choose to lead independently of each other, an unstable equilibrium with adverse consequences for the profit prospects of both will result. A price war, for instance, is possible in these circumstances. Likewise, if both leading firms choose to follow, we are back to the Cournot solution, since each firm is likely to take the other's output as given.

From this model, a dominant firm price-leadership situation can be depicted.[18] One large firm and a number of smaller firms are assumed. Let us assume that the dominant firm is able to estimate the sales of other competing firms in the industry under different market prices. With this assumption, the dominant firm is able to arrive at its own anticipated demand curve by deducting the other firms' sales from the anticipated industry's demand curve. Assuming further that there is information as to how its production costs are likely to vary with output, the dominant firm can select the price that maximizes its own profits. Other firms follow this price in an effort to maximize their profits or to enhance survivability.

Figure 1.2 demonstrates the case of dominant price leadership. DD' is the industry demand curve, and SS' is the small firms' supply curve. When market price is $0C$ where SS' intersects DD', small firms will be able to satisfy available demand. This is the price at which the dominant firm's demand curve cuts the vertical axis. At price $0S$ the small firms' supply will be zero so that the dominant firm's dD's are the same as the industry's demand curve, when price is below $0S$ and output beyond $0Y$. At price $0B$, the small

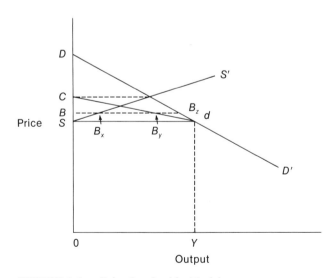

FIGURE 1.2.   Price Leadership Model

firms will be supplying BB_x, while the industry demand curve will be BB_z. By deducting a distance $B_yB_z = BB_x$ from the prevailing industry demand, the dominant firm will find BB_y of its product demanded when price is $0B$. Its demand curve will be CdD'.

Hence, the dominant firm's solution: It will derive its maximum price and output levels and therefore profits in the normal manner—that is, when marginal costs are equal to marginal revenue. If costs of production are the same for all the firms, the dominant firm can restrict the market growth of smaller firms and the entry of potential competitors. In the former case, it is able to retain a given market share and therefore its position of dominance; in the latter case, it can erect barriers to entry given its size advantage and its ability to determine the rules of the game of a given market. If one assumes economies of scale are being reaped by the dominant firm and that it therefore faces a lower average cost curve than its smaller rivals, its ability to determine the rules of the game of the market and to keep competition at a minimum are even greater. Empirical examples of dominant price leadership have been identified by a number of researchers.[19] Stigler has produced some evidence of barometric price leadership in oligopolistic types of markets.[20] Here the price leader is not necessarily the dominant or largest firm; the important consideration is that the firm takes the initiative in charging prices at levels that other firms find acceptable—hence, barometric. The point is that provided the price leader consistently sets prices at levels that other firms find satisfactory, it is likely to be acknowledged as the price leader regardless of its size.

Reference is sometimes made in the literature to collusive price leadership. Collusive price leadership, as defined by Markham, involves two conditions.[21] The first condition is that firms accept that they are better off by cooperating in price policy within a given market rather than pursuing divergent and competitive pricing decisions. Second, there is an absence of close substitutes. The purpose behind price collusion is joint profit maximization. However, under collusive price leadership, firms do not formally collude in determining the market prices; they merely follow a price leader. In this sense, a tacit form of collusion is operative.

Harrod and others have applied the use of pricing under oligopoly in relation to entry forestalling.[22] The argument here is that instead of setting prices that maximize short-run profits, firms would be inclined to set a price that yielded normal revenue so as to discourage new entrants and thereby reduce competition. Figure 1.3 shows a case of entry-forestalling pricing. New entrants' average and marginal costs are assumed to be $0B$. Existing firms' average and marginal costs are $0A$. Thus, by setting prices below $0B$, existing firms, through collusive pricing, are able to forestall new entrants.

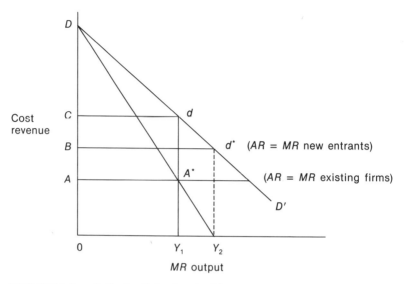

FIGURE 1.3. Collusive Price Leadership

These forms of market agreements, both tacit and open, tend to throw some reservations on the kinked demand curve depicting oligopoly pricing behavior. The argument developed by Hall and Hitch, on the one hand, and Sweezy, on the other, is that the kink comes about because if the oligopolist cuts prices, other firms in the industry will follow suit rather than see their market share being eroded.[23]

Conversely, if a firm raises its prices, others will not follow, preferring instead to gain from the price differentials, thereby increasing their market share and thus their profits. The demand curve will therefore exhibit a kink at the ruling market price—relatively inelastic for price falls and relatively elastic for price increases. On the other hand, the kinked demand curve has been used to explain price rigidity under oligopolistic conditions. It could be argued that tacit price agreement is limited only to the ruling market price because of the nature of the demand curve facing each oligopolist. Other ranges of price agreements are ruled out by the reaction function of other firms. Some critics have objected to this price-rigidity hypothesis on the basis of empirical findings.[24] Others, however, have extended the model to accommodate forms of price leadership.[25]

Simon and others have used behavioral theories to explain the behavior of firms in oligopoly types of markets and have suggested that instead of seeking only to maximize profits, firms normally satisfice[26]—that is, they seek a satisfactory level of profits, product quality, sales maximization, market share, a secure inventory base, and the like. This model could be interpreted as pointing to new dimensions that restrictive business practices may take in terms of the goals of firms. For example, it is conceivable that to secure inventory, a firm may restrict other firms' activities from the input side. This has been a common practice of vertically integrated mining companies.[27] Market sharing has been found relevant in recent cases of dominant firms' seeking to consolidate and to extend market power in an effort to build a business empire.[28]

A major shortcoming of these models of gross market imperfection is that they fail to take into account the dynamics of market life—for example, the emergence of oligopolies in the first instance. It is often assumed that such market power is autonomous. What are the main strategies adopted by firms to foster monopolistic control? Most of the theoretical discussion has been confined to pricing; yet it seems that other aspects of corporate strategy are also relevant. As Aaronovitch and Sawyer have recently argued, in terms of the conventional theory of the firm, "monopoly is just assumed to happen, and no clues are given to the circumstances under which it is likely to appear, or to those under which it is likely to collapse."[29] The same would seem applicable to oligopolies.

A dynamic approach to competition involving oligopoly types of firms could, however, be found within the Schumpeterian framework.[30] For Schumpeter, competition within the modern capitalist economy is essentially a process of creative destruction, of constant innovation by firms in search of more efficient methods of producing goods and services and creating new products. "The fundamental impulse that sets and keeps the capitalist engine in motion comes from the new consumers' goods, new methods of production, in transportation, new markets, new forms of industrial organization that the capitalist enterprise creates."[31] Schumpeter argues that this impulse "incessantly revolutionizes the economic structure from within, incessantly destroying the old one, incessantly creating a new one. This process of Creative Destruction is the essential fact about capitalism."[32]

Schumpeter attributed the effectiveness of this competitive process to the role of big business. Progress, he argued, is most conspicuous not "under conditions of comparatively free competition but precisely at the doors of large concerns."[33]

A number of economists have argued in support of the foregoing position. For example, Galbraith has argued that "a benign Providence has made the modern industry of a few large firms an almost perfect instrument for inducing technical change."[34] Hunter has suggested that "the days when one individual's inventiveness and enterprise could transform an industry are in the past. In this context, the big firm shows an advantage."[35]

A survey by a group of economists on the sources of modern innovation has brought some empirical evidence in support of the Schumpeterian position.[36] The study showed a decreasing importance of small firms in the innovative process over the past decades. In the words of the authors, "The novelty of this century [twentieth century] appears to be in the relative decline of the invention of the individual types. . . ."[37] The importance of individual invention associated with the names of Watt, Bessember, Edison, Daimler, and Benz has been overshadowed by the growing importance of large concerns in the innovation process, especially in such modern technology industries as electronics, chemicals, and engineering.[38]

Other writers, such as Clark, Downie, and Kantzenbach, have indeed drawn attention to the need to see competition as a dynamic process rather than a static one.[39]

BUSINESS CONCENTRATION AND THE REAL WORLD

With the foregoing background, we can proceed to see how the structure of gross market imperfection fits into the real-world situation.

Several economists have drawn attention to the large-scale nature of present-day business enterprises and the growing concentration of economic power found in modern capitalistic economies.[40] Modern corporations, Galbraith argues, are characterized by bigness.[41] Size is not necessarily indicative of concentration, especially if the minimum efficiency level for plants in a given industry gives rise to large firms rather than small ones being typical for the industry. However, evidence suggests that concentration does play a large role in setting the foundation for industrial expansion, and therefore firm size, in many instances.[42] Such concentration is particularly found among buyers, sellers, and producers in markets in Europe, the United States, and Japan.[43]

Several approaches are possible to calculate concentration ratios. Sales, value added, employment, and assets are some of the variables often used. The most widely used measure is the concentration ratio that measures levels of absolute concentration. For example, a simple ratio of the proportion of total industry output accounted for by a group of the largest firms (three or four) would be regarded as the concentration ratio of that industry. Another measure is the Lorenz curve. The further the Lorenz curve is from the line of equal distribution, the greater the concentration of firms in the industry. To this end, the Gini coefficient could be regarded as the concentration coefficient, though in strict terms it will measure the extent to which firms in the industry are of unequal size. Hence, it is often used as a measure of relative concentration. Logarithmic variance is also used as a measure of inequality or relative concentration among firms in a given industry.

A recent study by the Organization for Economic Cooperation and Development (OECD) indicated that one of the main features of industrial concentrations in industrialized countries is the growth of mergers.[44] The thesis advanced was that mergers have enabled firms to extend their market power in particular economies, thus enabling them to influence market conduct.[45] The main forms of mergers were identified as vertical, conglomerate, and horizontal. Other evidence suggests the rising importance of the first two types within recent years.

Among the reasons found in the literature for industrial concentration are increase in market power, empire building, promotional profits, economies of scale including learning by doing, the acquisition of capacity at reduced prices, use of complementary resources, risk spreading, tax reasons, and the like.[46] An analysis of these reasons is outside the scope of this study.

A few examples suffice to show the broad trend toward growing concentration and/or the presence of gross market imperfections in some developed countries. In the case of the Federal Republic of Germany, the market share of the largest 100 industrial enterprises rose from 34 percent in 1954 to 50 percent in 1969.[47] In Germany, mergers must be registered with the Federal Cartel Office when they meet certain market criteria—for example, if they jointly or singly control 20 percent of the market, employ 10,000 or more workers, or have annual sales proceeds of DM 500 million or more.[48] In 1958, only 15 enterprises' met these notification criteria; in 1973, the number rose to 242.[49] At the same time, substantial mergers rose from 16 in 1968 to 75 in 1972.[50] Recent estimates suggest that the biggest 50 enterprises, which constitute 0.001 percent of the total number of firms, account for over 40 percent of industry turnover.[51] The situation has led an OECD study to conclude that ''in respect of both the trend and the degree concentration, Germany has now outpaced all the other members of the European community.''[52]

Three major merger waves can be distinguished in the United States —1887–1905, 1916–1929, and post–World War II. In the first wave, horizontal mergers are reported to have played a major role in increased concentration. In the last two waves, vertical and conglomerate waves have been the main determinants of growing concentration.[53] However, precise data are not available on the relative incidence of these merger types on growing concentration in the United States over the years. During the first wave, some 15 percent of the total labor force and plants in the manufacturing sector was estimated to have been involved.[54] Some 3,000 independent firms disappeared, "the greater majority being in consolidation of 5 firms or more."[55] The second wave is reported to have involved some 12,000 firms.[56] Scant evidence suggests that the impact was not so great in terms of market concentration in the private sector as was the first wave; merger activity was heavily concentrated in the public utilities sector, so that the effect in terms of concentration in the private sector was not so great as the evidence on firm disappearance at first suggests.[57] We do not have precise data on the degree to which disappearing firms have been consolidated by larger ones, but the fact that the term *mergers for oligopoly* has been used to describe this merger wave tends to suggest that the incidence of consolidation was probably significant. During the post–World War II period, the Federal Trade Commission (FTC) recorded 11,668 mergers in manufacturing and mining between 1945 and 1965, with a rising incidence of mergers over the years. Thus, between 1966 and 1968, some 4,933 mergers were reported, so that on average the annual rate was 2,460. In comparison, the annual rate of mergers between 1945 and 1965 was 583.[58] Available data on firm size suggest that the acquired firms "were considerably smaller than the acquiring," which indicates that dominant firms had been playing an active role in merger activity.[59] Further, a substantial proportion of conglomerate mergers were reported. The situation led an expert group on restrictive business practices to conclude that "the consequence of this change has almost certainly been an increase in the level of concentration in the United States economy. . . ."[60] This conclusion is supported by data showing that in 1970 the overall concentration measured by the share of total value added held by the largest 100 companies had risen from 30 percent in 1954 to 33 percent.[61] In the United Kingdom, the share of manufacturing net output held by the largest 100 firms rose to 41 percent in 1972 compared with 26 percent in 1953 and 16 percent in 1909.[62] Merger activity was said to be responsible to an important extent for this increased concentration. For example, merger activity was concentrated among the largest corporations—the largest 120 corporations being responsible for 50 percent of the mergers. This affected two-thirds of the total assets involved in merger activity. At the same time, the 10 largest companies were involved in one-sixth of the mergers, and 6 percent of the largest companies accounted for 50 percent of the mergers and 66 percent of the total assets involved in merger activity.[63] The trend toward conglomerate mergers has been identified.

Data from the European Economic Community (EEC) suggest that between 1962 and 1970, the yearly number of business concentrations increased from 173 to 612.[64] A number of large-scale firms were said to have been involved. The situation has led some industrial economists to doubt the effectiveness of the EEC competition policy.[65]

A similar trend in growing market concentration has been noted in other OECD countries, including France and Japan. Some studies have shown that conglomerate mergers now play a substantial role in the growing concentration found in a large cross section of OECD countries.[66] In the meantime, evidence from Japan suggests that concentration is high in both sellers' and buyers' markets. In 1972, ten leading trading houses (Sogo Shoshas) accounted for 50 percent of that country's export sales and 60 percent of its import purchases.[67] However, concentration is also reported to be increasing in terms of industrial production. In this respect, the growing sellers' and buyers' concentration could be viewed as an organic feature of an overall concentration process.

Further, in the international economy, a recent OECD study shows the presence of a fair amount of cartel activity in some main industrialized countries.[68] For example, 70 export cartels were reported in Germany, 178 in Japan, 14 in the Netherlands, 130 in the United Kingdom, and 38 in the United States. The situation has led the OECD Expert Group on Restrictive Business Practices to call for the establishment of appropriate notification procedures for export cartels and international mergers.[69]

Even these data, albeit incomplete, seem to support Kaldor's observation that chains of oligopolies comprise the whole market[70] and Galbraith's contention that "oligopoly is the appropriate assumption. . . ."[71] The typology of oligopoly certainly gives rise to a number of questions such as the question of the changing structure of the firm (for instance, conglomerate and vertical instead of horizontal) and its justification as a result of technological demands of modern production processes, among other things. Our purpose is not to discuss these points; however, one point seems clear—that is, that dominant firms tend to play an increasing role in the economies of many developed economies.

We have already made reference to some of the adverse consequences that theory predicts will be brought about by forms of gross market imperfection. There is some dispute over the way this theory behaves in practice. As we saw, Schumpeter has argued that progress is most pronounced under conditions of gross market imperfection.[72] According to this position, the large-scale dominant-firm type revolutionizes the economic structure, gives dynamism to modern capitalist societies, and creates new methods of production, new products, and the like.[73] Be that as it may, a number of empirical studies have to some extent given support to theoretical predictions. Most of these studies are based on performance, and the criteria often used are industry profit rates, technical efficiency, technical progressiveness, and private profits of firms before and after increased concentration through mergers. Kipling found that increased concentration led to no economic benefits within a two-year period in 45 percent of the cases, and in the remaining 55 percent, executives concluded that they saw no special benefits in the immediate future.[74] Reid's study of 478 firms from *Fortune's* list of 500 of the largest U.S. industrial corporations in 1951 produced some interesting findings.[75] Firms that grew internally did poorly in terms of sales growth. However, they did better than merger-prone groups in terms of returns to shareholders, which is often used as an index of profitability. It is possible that merger-prone groups had been sacrificing short- or medium-term profitability in terms of long-run profitability. This possibility was not supported by the evidence, however. Singh conducted a study of performance on firms before and after concentration.[76] These results showed that on average 60–65 percent of the firms taken over had profitability, growth, and valuation ratios below their industry average. Further, 57 percent of the merged firms had a postacquisition profit that was less than the record of the separate firms before increased concentration.

Meek, in a study of concentration via mergers, coined the term *disappointing marriage* on the basis of the poor performance of these firms.[77] Meek and Whittington have likewise shown that increased concentration is associated not only with questionable corporate performance but also with important social costs' giving rise to concern.[78] O'Brien has also argued that the conventional explanations for the growth of concentration were unconvincing when looked at in real terms. He pointed out that the effects of scale economies, need to innovate, learning, and countervailing power hardly held. Similar findings have emerged from Pickering.[79] Jewkes, Sawers, and Stillerman have shown that key innovations are by no means wholly associated with large established firms.[80] Similar findings have recently been reported in *A Review of Monopolies and Merger Policy*.[81] The OECD in a recent investigation also concluded that "increased concentration beyond certain points results in allocative inefficiency."[82] This investigation raised questions concerning technical progress within concentrated industries, profitability, and social gain.[83] Social costs, argued the investigators, were not automatically offset by private gain.

Also, a recent finding noted that a "concentration of control is not exclusively and probably even primarily related to technological change but to attempts to obtain and retain monopolistic market conditions."[84] Cowling and Mueller have argued that previous studies on monopolies have underestimated the adverse consequences of monopoly type of situations because they have failed to take into account resources wasted in the "creation of market power and its protection."[85]

MARKET POWER AND THE LAW

A factor associated with the rising industrial concentrations in industrial economies is the increasing vigilance of monopoly authorities in respective countries and the enforcement of laws to regulate the control of restrictive business practices. These regulations include attempts to control merger activity where it leads to market dominance or forms of collusiveness. Chapter 4 reviews some of these laws.

We cannot determine with precision whether the growing public concern over restrictive business practices is the result of increasing concentration or a better recognition of the problems associated with concentration.[86] Increased public awareness is no doubt partly a function of the growing importance of restrictive business practices in economic life. Therefore, we could argue that the changing structure of modern business—namely, its size, complexity, and ability to control markets—is an important consideration.[87]

2 LITERATURE ON DEVELOPMENT

Since we intend to discuss restrictive business practices within the context of development, we will do well to start by reviewing the existing literature. Three main time periods of thinking are observable. They are not mutually exclusive. They are (1) the approaches of the 1950s and early 1960s, (2) the structural and international theories of the 1960s and 1970s, and (3) the transdisciplinary approaches of the 1970s. Before we look at them, we will take a brief conceptual look at growth and development.

GROWTH AND DEVELOPMENT

In its simplified form, economic development may be regarded as sustained increases in real output—namely, growth that is in turn translated into improvements in human welfare. Such increases could be depicted by means of an ordinary transformation curve. If it is argued in theory that restrictive business practices limit the growth of output in an economy, for example, clearly this aspect is relevant to a discussion of development. Yet, as we will see, the literature on development shows the absence of any systematic treatment of the subject.

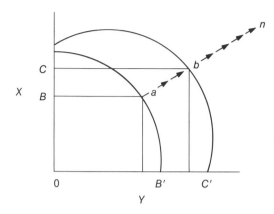

FIGURE 2.1.   Transformation Possibilities

Figure 2.1 shows increases in real output from 0*B* of *X* and 0*B'* of *Y* to 0*C* of *X* and 0*C'* of *Y* at respective optimum points—namely, *a* to *b*. This higher optimum point is the result of a shift in the transformation curve over time. If constant population is assumed and favorable distribution assumptions are made, it is safe to further assume that the increase in real output goes to the benefit of improvements in social welfare for the population. The change in output just described could be brought about by one of the following considerations or some combination thereof: an increase in the quantity of capital, improvements in the quality of labor, technical improvements to capital, discovery of new sources of materials, or better organization of factors of production as a result of *X* efficiency.[1] Progressive increases in real output will be possible, and growth self-sustaining, if the changes just referred to are continuous. See the distance *a* to *n* in Figure 2.1.

It is also possible to use more sophisticated constructs, such as formal growth models of the Harrod Dormar steady-state type or von Neumann turnpike models, to demonstrate these processes at work. However, that is not really necessary for our immediate purpose. As Hicks has reminded us, it is an error to associate formal growth theory with the problem of underdevelopment.[2]

THE 1950s TO THE EARLY 1960s

In a general sense, it could be said that the history of development economics could be traced to political economy. A primary concern of some of the 1950s/1960s analyses of development is the determination of factors leading to long-term growth prospects of nations. This was in fact a main concern of Adam Smith when he wrote *An Inquiry into the Nature and Causes of the Wealth of Nations* in 1776.[3] Smith's basic argument can be summarized as follows: Division of labor was the key to increased productivity and therefore to growth. However, division of labor could not take place on any appreciable scale unless labor had access to specialized machinery and equipment. Smith emphasized the need for an economy to accumulate stocks of capital goods in order to enjoy the fruits of higher per capita incomes—capital accumulation in a given economy being determined by the overall propensity to save. Further, division of labor was limited by the market size. If markets were too small, demand would not be forthcoming to produce goods under specialized production methods; hence, the gains from specialization would be limited.

Other people saw the problem rather differently. For example, corn (and therefore the agricultural sector) was of special concern to Ricardo.[4] Here land—namely, its scarcity—is an important constraint for augmenting agriculture and national output.[5] The important capital in Ricardo's model is corn inputs needed for further agricultural production. In this model, profits are assumed to be largely saved and invested, and wages are assumed to be consumed; the share of profits in income would govern the share of investment in total production and the rate of capital accumulation. The rate of capital accumulation is in turn assumed to determine the rate of increase in employment of labor since employment is assumed to grow at the same rate as capital. Kaldor has argued that little inquiry was made into the source of additional labor supplies, but he reminds us that the model is somewhat consistent with the assumptions of unlimited labor supply.[6] The subject of unlimited supplies of labor was to occupy a central place in the treatment of underdevelopment in the 1950s, as we will soon see.

Malthus, for instance, saw the growth of population as the central factor inhibiting economic growth. The reason for this, argued Malthus, was that population increased geometrically, while food supply increased arithmetically. Because of this disproportionality problem, the gains from real output were swallowed up by population growth.[7] In a world in which food supply was not only wage goods but also capital (inventories for further production of food), this would reduce capital accumulation and therefore reduce long-term growth prospects.

Meanwhile, in the 1930s, the role of the entrepreneur as a key factor in the development process was stressed by Schumpeter, who was cited earlier in a different context.[8] Basically, the entrepreneur's function was seen to be of an innovative nature—namely, finding new uses for factor combinations and products. For example, this function included the introduction of new commodities on the market, utilization of new production methods, opening up of new market areas, development of new sources of raw material supplies, industrial reorganization, and the like. For Schumpeter, development involved significant economic changes. Entrepreneurs, because they were basically change-oriented, were assumed to be the main agents in this process.

These attempts were of a more or less general nature. From the 1950s, the focus of development analysis for the first time became a treatment of problems specific to developing countries. The central question was: Why were most countries in Africa, Asia, Latin America, and the Caribbean "underdeveloped," while most of those in Europe and North America were "developed"? The main criteria for defining underdevelopment were real per capita income levels, literacy rates, incidence of poverty, real growth rates, levels of unemployment, and monoculturally biased economies.

Let us piece together some of the main themes of this early period. One of these was the dualistic interpretation of development. Thus, W. A. Lewis, one of the chief protagonists of this theory, saw the problem as one of intersectoral adjustments.[9] Two main sectors are assumed to exist—a subsistence sector and a capitalist sector. The latter is defined as that part of the economy using reproducible capital, paying capitalists for the use of this capital, and employing wage labor—for example, in mines, on plantations, and in factories. The former sector is that part of the economy not using reproducible capital. It is also characterized by "unlimited" supplies of labor with extremely low and even negative marginal productivity—for example, peasant agriculture. The main problem of development is promoting the expansion of the modern exchange economy; this is so because the modern sector is considered the propellant for capital formation and therefore for development. When the capitalist sector expands, it is assumed to draw the surplus labor from the subsistence sector. Given the complementarity between capital and labor, the surplus labor acts as a safety valve for industrial expansion. However, this surplus labor has to be induced to move. The wage rate is determined by the opportunity cost of labor—namely, what it earns in the subsistence sector. The point is, however, that peasants will not leave the family farm for wage employment unless the real wage is at least as high as the average product on the land. Crucial to the whole development process, according to Lewis, is the use that the capitalist makes of surplus or profits. The driving force of the system is the reinvestment of the capitalist surplus in the creation of new capital. As capital accumulation marches ahead, a continuous process of labor absorption is set in motion to facilitate the progressive expansion of productive capital, profits are further reinvested, and the process of development continues. Variants of the Lewis model have been developed subsequently by other economists.[10] The Lewis model could be interpreted as a takeoff of the Ricardian tradition. However, the source of surplus is a more integral feature of the Lewis model.[11] Lewis himself has reminded us, however, that he was writing precisely in the classical tradition.[12]

Higgins and Ekaus in a slightly different vein attempted to give a technological content to dualism—namely, the use of different production functions in the advanced sector and the traditional sector.[13] Basically, the peasant sector was seen as having among its characteristics peasant agriculture, handicrafts or very small industries, and factor endowments favoring labor-intensive techniques of production. In contrast, the modern sector was seen to have very limited technical substitutability of factors of production so that the production function was characterized by fixed technical coefficients of production. The production process here was marked by capital-intensive techniques. The rural sector was considered to be the only source of surplus labor. This surplus labor arose because of the low marginal productivity of labor.

Writing earlier, Boeke attempted to offer a social interpretation of dualism.[14] The problem was seen as the existence of an imported, modern social system coexisting with an indigenous and traditional social system. Most frequently, Boeke observed, the imported social system was highly capitalist, while the indigenous system was largely precapitalist in nature.

An early thesis frequently advanced for underdevelopment was the so-called vicious circle.[15] The problem was seen in the following terms: Poverty meant low productivity, and that meant low incomes. This tended to bring about low saving rates, given the high marginal propensity to consume among low-income earners, or Engels Law, as it has come to be known in economics. Low savings in turn meant low levels of investment, which in turn accounted for the deficiency of capital found. Since savings were necessary for investment and investment was necessary for real output, savings were looked upon as both a cause and effect of poverty. Other considerations were that low incomes were insufficient to provide minimum nutritional needs for the population. The effect of this consideration was to impair physical efficiency, which brought about low real output levels, thereby perpetuating poverty. In this sense, the problem can be considered to be one of human capital formation.

Another idea of the vicious-circle thesis related to the role of demand in capital formation. The position was taken that poverty implied a low level of aggregate demand, which in turn explained why there was low profitability among firms and therefore limited investment—the inducement to investment being negligible.

Rostow, in popularizing the so-called stages approach to development, noted that economies could be characterized by five stages: (1) traditional society, (2) preconditions for takeoff, (3) the takeoff, (4) the drive to maturity, and (5) the age of mass consumption.[16] The traditional society was seen as one with limited production functions. Pre-Newtonian techniques of production and traditional attitudes were prevalent—hence, the static nature of these societies. A very high proportion of resources was devoted to agriculture. Manufacturing was not ruled out, but "as in agriculture the level of productivity was limited by the accessibility of modern science and technology, its application and its frame of mind."[17]

The takeoff was seen as "the interval when old blocks and resistance to steady growth are fully overcome."[18] This was the period of rapid industrial expansion, high profits, high savings, and rapid economic transformation. In Rostow's words:

During the takeoff new industries expand rapidly, yielding profits, a large proportion of which are reinvested in new plants, and these new industries in turn stimulate, through their rapidly expanding requirement for factory workers, the services to support them, and for other manufactured goods, a further expansion in urban areas and in other modern industrial plants. The whole process of expansion in the modern sector yields an increase of income in the hands of those who not only save at high rates but place their savings at the disposal of those engaged in modern sector activities. The new class of entrepreneurs expands, and it directs the enlarging flows of investment into the private sector. The economy exploits hitherto unused natural resources and methods of production.[19]

The preconditions for this takeoff were to a large extent exogenously determined. "Insights of modern science began to be translated into new production functions in both agriculture and industry, in a setting given dynamism by the lateral expansion of world markets and international competition for them. . . ."[20]

To arrive at maturity meant reaching a phase when a progressively higher proportion of national income is allocated to investment—namely, between 10 and 20 percent. This provides further potential stimulus for growth of real output. The structure of the economy undergoes further changes in terms of production techniques and level of industrialization. The economy then becomes competitive internationally; there is successful import substitution as domestic markets expand, and new export sectors emerge.[21] The age of mass consumption represents further complexity in the structure of production. The leading sectors shift toward durable consumer goods and services and automated type of production.[22]

Apart from these, other explanations existed for the state of socioeconomic backwardness. One was the population trap. Rapid population growth was seen as a main cause of underdevelopment. However, Hirschman, following a position advanced earlier by Hicks, has argued against this Malthusian standpoint.[23] Growth of population from this position is regarded as a stimulus to development. For example, it induces investment in social overhead capital, such as hospitals, schools, public amenities, and so on. It also results in a greater supply of labor, which increases the human capital potential of an economy. Also, a larger population means a potentially greater effective demand. Another explanation was climatic considerations, as advanced by Bauer and Yamey. Extreme climate, it was argued, adversely affects energy and motivation of the population and induces a state of comparative poverty.[24] Other writers, such as Schultz, stressed the importance of education in economic development, especially in view of the high illiteracy rates that exist in developing countries. This in turn was connected with the problem of inadequate supply of skills in such countries.

While it is true that little systematic attempt was made at dealing with the development problem in terms of noneconomic factors, attempts were made at offering what can be considered largely sociological explanations—for example, insecurity, childhood training, attitudinal characteristics, and the like.[25]

INTERNATIONAL ASPECTS

The 1960s saw a different thrust in the treatment of development—namely, a shift to what might be called *structural* and *international* considerations.[26] Myrdal, for example, argued that underdevelopment is not an isolated phenomenon.[27] It is in fact part of a world process in which powerful nations have impoverishing effects on other parts. Myrdal described this debilitating effect of world economic relations as "backwash effects." This position ran against conventional trade theory. Classical economic theory held that trade based on comparative advantage would ensure that the benefits of world division of labor would spread and that the free movement of goods, capital, and labor would prevent backwardness. Myrdal, however, pointed out that in the absence of counteracting measures, trade will not move toward an equalization of world incomes. His argument was that trade strengthens the rich and progressive countries whose manufacturing industries have the lead and are already fortified by the surrounding economies, while the underdeveloped countries are in continuous danger of seeing even what they have of industry, and in particular of small-scale industry and handicrafts, priced out by cheap imports from industrialized countries.[28]

The main positive effect of international trade, according to this view, is the specialization of production of primary products employing mainly unskilled labor. However, since primary products often meet with inelastic price and income demands in the export markets, the argument was that they do not usually promote development; thus, trade and primary production strengthen the process of stagnation or regression in developing countries.

Kindleberger had earlier produced evidence on the deterioration of the barter terms of trade between developing countries and the industrialized ones.[29] Also, Cairncross showed that the world demand of poor countries' export products during the greater part of the twentieth century had tended to increase much less in proportion to the production and income of the developed countries.[30] This position was further established by other economists, such as Baldwin and Prebisch.[31]

The role of developing countries in the world division of labor and the disadvantages assumed to be associated with it—namely, poor growth and development prospects—led to the advocacy for structural diversification of these economies.[32] In this context, much stress was laid on manufacturing activities as a means of accelerating growth and development.[33] For example, the formation of UNCTAD in the 1960s saw the setting up of an international forum in which the acceleration of developing countries' exports of manufactured goods was considered to be a top priority.[34] It was held that the potential for manufactured exports of developing countries to developed countries faced various forms of tariffs and nontariff barriers to trade. Much of UNCTAD's work has been centered on reducing these barriers.

Some writers held that foreign aid should be encouraged so as to augment limited resources in developing countries—for instance, to provide infrastructure necessary for industrialization, training in industrial and other skills, and the provision of capital necessary for development.[35] These writers were not without critics who argued that foreign aid, especially that of a bilateral nature, was tied politically and economically, thereby preventing recipient countries from using aid under terms optimal from their point of view.

A similar gap-filling hypothesis was put forward for foreign private capital and the role of transnational firms.[36] Developing countries needed to industrialize, and industrial skills, entrepreneurial talent, capital, marketing, and management were held to be virtually nonexistent in developing countries. Foreign capital with its comparative advantage in these resources could therefore be a harmonious partner in the development efforts of developing countries. For example, Lewis strongly advanced the case for industrialization in the Caribbean along these lines. It was grounded empirically in the Puerto Rican industrial development experience of the 1940s and later. Lewis contended that the small size of domestic markets in the Caribbean meant that these economies had to be competitive internationally in manufactured goods in order to benefit from self-sustained growth. Barbados, Singapore, Brazil, Kenya, Mexico, and Taiwan are among the countries to have followed this strategy consistently over the years.

But the case for foreign capital in economic development, however plausible it seemed under theoretical grounds, was to become a major source of criticism from the "dependency school," which emerged in Latin America and the Caribbean.[37] The central thesis of this school was that economic dependency was the root cause of underdevelopment. Such dependency, ran the argument, was brought about by the world division of labor that had its roots in colonialism. A main feature of this division was the subordination of peripheral economies to metropolitan economies. One aspect of the subordination was the specialization by developing countries in primary products geared largely to satisfy the demand of industrialized countries. According to this school, the problem was further complicated by the control of such economies by foreign capital.[38]

The problem of underdevelopment was seen to be an interplay of political and economic forces. Surplus value, it was contended, was drained from Third World economies by foreign capital; very little processing took place in agriculture and mining, intersectoral linkages were virtually nonexistent, local value added was not optimized and political sovereignty was undermined, balance of payments was adversely affected, technology and skills transferred were not appropriate, and sociocultural distortions emerged.[39] Thus, Wionczek argued that "the efforts of foreign capital to perpetuate the political and economic dependence of Latin America on the industrial societies, particularly dependence on the United States, represent probably the single most important element in the growing conflict between foreign capital and Latin American society."[40]

Also, dependency on raw materials for exports (where market prospects were often considered to be unfavorable) and on imports of manufactured goods (which were held to be relatively highly priced), meant that developing countries not only found themselves in "unfavorable trading relationships" with the outside world but also that such countries found it difficult to break this form of international specialization, given the forces at work. Later attempts by developing countries at industrialization, ran the argument, resulted in new forms of penetration of foreign capital and a continuation of the state of dependency.[41] For the dependency school, therefore, the main solution to underdevelopment was the elimination of forms of economic control.[42]

In a similar but more radical vein, the Marxist version of this argument stressed the need for the socialization of means of production as well as the severing of international capitalist economic relationships.[43] For example, Frank, Amin, and Baran and Sweezy argued that the problem was not dependency as such but the nature of dependent capitalism. The road to development was a change in the mode of production; underdevelopment was the result of contradictions of world capitalism.[44] Central to the Baran and Sweezy analysis was the question of monopoly capitalism. Advanced capitalism needed overseas market outlets and raw materials for transformation into outputs as markets in metropolitan countries reached their critical limits.[45] This position was influenced by Lenin's analysis of imperialism as an extension of capitalism. A conservative version of this interpretation is found in Hobson's work.[46]

It is worth pointing out that the study of foreign capital was by no means confined to what might be regarded as the dependency school. Independent scholarly work emerged to encompass the study of the transnational firm.[47] This is probably not surprising given its inadequate theoretical treatment, on the one hand, and its relative novelty and growing importance in the world economy, on the other.[48] On the whole, however, the analysis of restrictive business practices remained a neglected field in the study of such corporations in the problem of underdevelopment. As we have argued elsewhere, the concept of restrictive business practices was often considered more as a matter of legal investigation than of development.[49] This position has been confirmed by a recent comprehensive United Nations study on transnational corporations in world development. The study failed to analyze the importance of restrictive business practices to development problems.[50] This failure may be considered surprising in view of the terms of reference of the study—namely, "to study the role of multinational corporations and their impact on the process of development, especially that of developing countries, and also their implications for international relations, to formulate conclusions which may possibly be used by governments in making their sovereign decisions regarding national policy in this respect. . . ."[51] On the other hand, UNCTAD's work on restrictive business practices does argue that such practices can have adverse effects on development prospects.[52]

Finally, the 1970s saw a new feature in the field of development thinking: the emergence of proposals for the establishment of a new international economic order between developed and developing countries.[53] The thesis advanced was for the real transfer of resources from developed to developing countries in order to improve development prospects of the latter. Central to this thesis was the transfer of capital and technology, better prices for

raw materials, and the control over operations of transnational corporations, among others.[54] A main aspect of this framework for development is
cooperation between developed and developing countries, collective self-reliance among developing countries, and a recognition of the interdependence of the world economic community.[55] The thesis could therefore be interpreted as one of international economic integration. Details are yet to be
worked out as to how the ideals can be operationalized.

TOWARD A SOCIAL SCIENTIFIC INTERPRETATION

Within recent years, the earlier approaches to development have come
under criticism. The basis for this criticism is largely methodological. The
economic interpretation that had characterized development thinking was
regarded as inadequate.[56] Instead, it was argued, development should be
seen conceptually as a part of a socioeconomic, political, and historical process.[57] One writer expresses the problem this way:

> Development is not a purely economic phenomenon. . . . Development should
> therefore be perceived as a multidimensional process involving the reorganization
> and reorientation of entire economic and social systems. In addition to improve-
> ments in incomes and output, it typically involves radical changes in institutional,
> social, and administrative structures, as well as in popular attitudes and some-
> times even customs and beliefs. Finally, although development is usually defined
> in a national context, its widespread realization may necessitate fundamental
> modifications of the international economic and social system.[58]

Seers and others had earlier stressed that it was a mistake to view development mainly in terms of per capita incomes and growth.[59] The standard view was that growth will automatically lead to development since it
will bring about material improvement in social welfare. However, the
problem of unemployment and inequality in incomes and wealth became
two issues that were used to illustrate that the growth process in many developing countries failed to solve some basic development problems. The
position was taken that

> unemployment was one of the main roots of inequality both directly and indi-
> rectly. Conversely, inequality promotes unemployment because of the tendency
> of the rich and of town dwellers to spend their incomes on luxuries which are im-
> ported or which incorporate a high import content, thus preempting the use of
> foreign exchange for capital equipment and thereby reducing the potential long-
> run growth of output and employment. Unemployment and inequality, however,

between them meant the persistence of poverty and of related evils such as ill health and illiteracy; these social evils also are in turn contributory causes to unemployment and inequality.[60]

In like manner, Griffin and others have drawn attention to the fact that rural development prospects in developing countries were adversely affected by the unevenness of social structures that limited access of poorer groups —namely, landless laborers, small-scale peasants, and the unemployed—to key economic resources. This difficulty in turn affected the distribution of income and social welfare in such countries.[61] A number of studies in Latin America, the Caribbean, and parts of Asia have supported these findings.[62]

A more recent attempt at incorporating interdisciplinary approaches to development is to be found in the basic-needs strategy enunciated by the International Labor Organization (ILO).[63] In essence, this strategy calls for an improvement in social-overhead capital in developing countries, concerted attempts at reducing poverty, access of the poor to public services, and popular participation in decision making and in the benefits of social wealth.[64] The thesis of this approach is that development strategies should be aimed at satisfying the basic needs of the human population.

CONCLUSION

This chapter represents mainly an attempt to illustrate in a more or less general manner some of the trends that have emerged in development thinking over the years. Our immediate concern, however, is that in spite of the growth of ideas on the subject, the existing body of development thinking has somehow failed to consider in a systematic manner the role of restrictive business practices in development.

3 RESTRICTIVE BUSINESS PRACTICES, TRANSNATIONAL CORPORATIONS, AND ASPECTS OF CONTROL

One of the principal characteristics of restrictive business practices of transnational corporations as they affect developing countries is the absence of effective legislative control. This chapter examines legislation in selected developed countries, accounting for most of the activities of transnational corporations in developing countries. An examination is also made of legislation relating to restrictive business practices in a specific group of developing countries.

LEGISLATION IN SELECTED DEVELOPED COUNTRIES

United States

Attempts to exercise control over restrictive business practices in the United States date back to the Sherman Act of 1890. The main restrictive business practices laws, in addition to the Sherman Act, are the Clayton Act (1914), the Federal Trade Commission Act (1914), and the Webb Pomerene Act (1918). After the American Civil War of 1865, the pattern of industrial organization in the United States underwent substantial changes. Between

1860 and 1890, for example, a substantial part of trade and industry came under the control of large industrial trusts. This control affected a number of important industries, such as petroleum, meat packing, sugar, lead, and coal.[1] By the 1880s these business trusts had created widespread public concern over their effects on competition. They later became a source of legal inquiry.[2]

Within this economic-legal context, the Sherman Act of 1890 emerged. The act has been described as "a comprehensive charter of economic liberty aimed at preserving free and unfettered competition as the rule of trade."[3] The principal substantive provisions of the Sherman Act are contained in Sections 1 and 2. Section 1 declares "every contract, combination, or conspiracy in restraint of interstate or foreign commerce to be illegal." Section 2 declares "monopolization, attempts to monopolize, interstate or foreign commerce to be illegal."[4] Dissatisfaction over the effectiveness of the Sherman Act, however, resulted in the passing of the three subsequent restrictive business practices laws mentioned earlier.

The Clayton Act spells out in detail restrictive business practices deemed to be legally intolerable. Section 2 of the act prohibits discrimination likely to adversely affect small business.[5] Section 3 was intended to eliminate restrictive business practices in the distribution trade.[6] For example, it attempted to ensure free access to distribution outlets by prohibiting tying practices (that is, refusal to sell or to lease one product unless another is taken with it) and exclusive dealing arrangements that may "substantially lessen competition or tend to create a monopoly in any line of commerce."[7] Section 7 was designed to eliminate anticompetitive mergers by prohibiting one corporation from acquiring the stock of another where the effect might be to substantially lessen competition between them.[8] And Section 8 sought to eliminate forms of collusive practices of competing corporations by prohibiting interlocking directorships.[9] In 1936 parts of the Clayton Act were amended by the Robinson-Patman Act. This act prohibits price discrimination between purchasers of similar commodities when the effect of discrimination "may be to substantially lessen competition or tend to create a monopoly in any line of commerce or may tend to injure competition with persons granting the discriminatory prices, those knowingly reserving the benefits of discrimination, or with customers of either of them."[10]

In 1950 parts of the Clayton Act were strengthened to improve the effectiveness of national legislation in the area of restrictive business practices. The main changes were that the act was made applicable to assets as well as to stock acquisitions. Prohibition was also expanded to cover all types of mergers that might substantially lessen competition.[11] These included vertical and conglomerate mergers, which were then on the rise. Antimerger

enforcement is a major part of present-day restrictive business practices policy in the United States. For example, in 1972, twenty-eight of the eighty-
seven restrictive business practices complaints filed by the Department of
Justice were for anticompetitive mergers.[12]

The Federal Trade Commission Act created the Federal Trade Commission (FTC). The purpose of that act was to set up an agency to administer
the competitive process. The two broad functions of the FTC are: (1) to
oversee unfair methods of competition and unfair or deceptive acts or practices in commerce, and (2) to investigate and report on economic problems
and corporate activity, especially in relation to restrictive business practices.[13]

Some exceptions to restrictive business practices legislation exist. The
main ones are collective labor activities under the Norris-LaGuardia Act
and the National Labor Relations Act, agricultural cooperatives by the
Capper Volstead Act of 1922, insurance by the McCarran Ferguson Act, resale price maintenance under the McGuire and Miller Tydings Act, and professional sports and natural monopolies.

Of special relevance to this study, however, is that under the Webb
Pomerene Act, the operations of associations of firms engaged in export
trade are exempted from the prohibitions on concerted action contained in
the Sherman Act, provided that no corresponding restraint on trade occurs
within the United States or on the export trade of any domestic competi-
tor.[14] Also, considerable leeway exists for national firms laws because some
firms are engaged in international production to escape regulation problems
concerning the extraterritorial application of national laws. This remains so
even though some recorded evidence shows that action has been taken
against such firms[15]—for example, the American Tobacco in 1927, Sisal
Sales Corporation in 1926, Union Carbide in 1962, United Fruit in 1909,
and Aluminum Company of America in 1962.[16] However, the main criterion for legal action against firms that operate internationally is whether
or not they have a substantial effect on American foreign commerce.[17] In
other words, national interests are the paramount concern.

United Kingdom

Some of the main restrictive business practices laws that have been enacted
include the Monopolies and Restrictive Business Practices Act of 1948, the
Restrictive Trade Practices Act of 1956, the Resale Prices Act of 1964, the
Agriculture and Forestry Associations Act of 1962, the Restrictive Trade

Practices Act of 1968, and the Fair Trading Act of 1973. These laws do not usually make special reference to U.K. transnational corporations that operate overseas.

The 1948 act, for example, provided for the setting up of a Monopolies and Restrictive Business Practices Commission to investigate and to report on matters concerning market abuse. These include conditions relating to the supply of goods where at least one-third of the market was supplied by "a single firm or by two or more firms acting together whether by agreement or not, in a manner restricting competition."[18] Similar provisions were made in relation to processing and export; however, in the latter area the commision has been virtually inactive. For example, between 1948 and 1955, only one report was filed in the field of exports.[19] Further, the 1948 act, under Section 14, gave guidance to the commission as to factors that should be taken into account in determining whether or not competition operated against the public interest.[20] The act was repealed by the Fair Trading Act of 1973, to which we return shortly. The 1956 Restrictive Business Practices Act reduced the scope of matters to be referred to the commission by excluding abandoned agreements, agreements relating to patents and trademarks, and agreements that were regarded as insignificant. Part 1 of the 1973 act also exempted agreements relating to export trade.[21] This tradition of noninterference in domestic firms' activities in international trade and investment has been a standing feature of British restrictive business practices tradition. For example, overseas investment and trade were actively encouraged as part of British colonial policy. More often than not these firms were leaders in the areas of shipping, insurance, banking, and primary-sector activities, including agriculture and mining.

Basically, the 1956 act made the commission responsible mainly for market conditions affecting the supply of goods where trade was dominated by a single firm. However, oligopolistic agreements can in principle be referred to the commission.

Under the Resale Prices Act of 1964, contractual conditions and arrangements intended to maintain minimum resale prices are considered unlawful. However, suppliers are not prohibited from recommending minimum resale prices.[22] Further, it is considered unlawful for the supplier to withhold goods from a dealer and to offer discriminatory terms of sale on the grounds that a dealer has not been observing minimum resale prices or recommended ones.

Further changes in the legislation took place in 1965 when the Monopolies and Merger Act was passed. The purpose of this act was to strengthen legislation over the control of monopolies, including those in the tertiary sector, which include mergers.[23] In particular, it involved instances in which mergers would lead to a strengthening of a monopoly or in which the gross value of assets taken over exceeded £5 million. A basic weakness of the act was that it subjected monopolies to administrative control rather than to judicial control. However, this act was repealed in 1973 when a further attempt was made to strengthen control over monopolies and forms of market dominance. Information agreements previously excluded from restrictive business practices control came under regulation in 1968 with the passing of the Restrictive Business Practices Act. However, under this act, agreements of substantial importance to the national economy are excluded from control, and the government is empowered to grant exemption if it is consistent with national incomes and price policy.[24]

The most recent attempt to consolidate restrictive business practices legislation in the United Kingdom is the 1973 Fair Trading Act. Consumer protection is now included as an important feature of restrictive business practices. The law also covers agreements in the supply of commercial and professional services.

Federal Republic of Germany

In the case of Germany, the main present-day provision for the control of restrictive business practices goes back to the Act against Restraints of Competition as amended in 1957. The tradition to control restrictive business practices in Germany, however, predates this act. For example, the Act Against Unfair Competition of 1909 regarded all acts committed in the course of business that are contrary to commercial morality as "unfair competition."[25] In 1933 the Act on Discounts and Rebates prohibited forms of rebates and discounts deemed harmful to competition. In 1954 the Act on Penalties for Economic Offenses prohibited "unreasonably high prices which are the result of restraint of competition, abuses of economic power, or shortages of supply."[26]

The 1957 act covers cartel agreements, market-dominating enterprises, restrictive and discriminatory conduct, competition rules, general provisions, and prohibition procedure. Section 1 of the act, dealing with cartels, states, "Agreements made for a common purpose by enterprises or associations of enterprises and decisions by associations of enterprises shall be of no effect, insofar as they are likely to influence, by restraining competition, production, or market condition with respect to trade in goods or commercial services."[27] Some provisions are made for exemptions. These are contained mainly in Sections 3–14. For instance, Section 3 makes exemption to rebates "insofar as such rebates represent a genuine compensation for services rendered and do not lead to unjustifiably discriminatory treatment of stages in the economic process or of customers."[28] Section 4 exempts agreements that are necessary "to bring about a planned adjustment of productive capacity to the demand and if the arrangement takes into consideration the overall economy and the public interest."[29] Section 5 does not apply to agreements dealing with the uniform application of standards and types.[30] Section 5a allows agreements whose object is to rationalize economic activities and specialization provided that "substantial competition continues to exist in the market."[31]

Relevant for our purpose are Sections 6 and 7 of the act. These exempt agreements that serve "to protect and promote exports." Import cartels are permissible if German importers are faced with monopolistic or oligopolistic competition on the foreign suppliers' side. The agreements must not, however, relate to transactions on the domestic market, "but indirect domestic effects necessarily arising out of [their] performance do not prevent authorization."[32]

A number of restrictive business practices are allowed as they affect patents. These include the following:

Restrictions imposed upon the acquirer or licensee;
Obligations with respect to prices charged for the protected article;
Obligations of the licensee to exchange experience or to grant license for improvement;
Obligation of the acquirer not to challenge the protected right;
Obligations relating to the regulation of competition in markets.[33]

At the same time Sections 25–27 on restrictive and discriminatory conduct prohibit enterprises or associations of enterprises from coercing other enterprises to:

Join an agreement;
Merge with other enterprises;
Act uniformly in the market with intent to restrain competition.

Additionally, refusals to sell or to purchase, price fixing, and differential treatment are prohibited in Germany.

In relation to market-dominating enterprises, merger control may prohibit mergers if at least 20 percent of the market share is obtained.

France

The interest in France in regulating unfair competition goes back to 1791. At that time, an act was passed forbidding citizens to act collusively, in respect of their "pretended common interest."[34] Further, Article 419 of the Criminal Code of 1810 prohibited illicit speculation and the pursuit of profits that did not arise out of free competition.[35] Up to the present time, contravention of restrictive business practices regulation is regarded as criminal.

According to a survey by the OECD, the main provisions presently in force in France for the control of restrictive business practices are to be found in the following decrees:

The amended Decree of August 1959 and the Ordinance of September 1967;
Articles 3 and 4 of the Finance Act of July 1963.[36]

This view is probably correct since the earlier attempts had evolved into a consistent set of measures aimed at regulating abuse arising from forms of gross market imperfections. The recent regulations since 1953 could be divided into two broad sets of provisions. The first deals with prohibitions. The following are among the forms of market conduct prohibited:

Refusal to sell when buyers' request is normal;
Unjustifiable commercial discrimination and price differences exceeding those specified by government;
Making sales conditional on the purchase of other goods or of a minimum quantity;
Minimum resale prices except those allowed by government.

The other set of provisions deals with combines and dominant market positions. In this regard, the prohibited agreements include agreements relating to market sharing, production or selling quotas, and price-fixing clauses, among others.[37] Special exemptions are made for agreements when these result in "the expansion of economic progress, in particular increasing productivity."[38] However, a prior condition for this exemption is a detailed government investigation.

The French approach to restrictive business practices concentrates largely on the domestic market, and as a general rule activities of national enterprises in the international economy, including exports, are not subject to regulation. For example, such exemptions are granted under Article 62 of the Ordinance of 1967.[39] However, a number of cartels affecting domestic economic activity, such as the Franco-Belgian cartel for road-making materials and cartels among importers of Nordic wood, shippers, and forwarding agents, have been brought before the Technical Commission on Combines and Dominant Positions.[40]

The Netherlands

Restrictive business practices legislation has a relatively recent history in the Netherlands. The main laws are the 1935 Entrepreneurs' Agreements Act, the Cartel Decree of 1941, the Business Agreements Suspension Act of 1951, and the Economic Competition Act of 1956.

The 1935 act was intended to promote forms of business cooperation and to put an end to cutthroat competition. The rationale for the law was that such competition prevented "efficient firms from recovering their costs."[41] In these circumstances, agreements between entrepreneurs to normalize competition became legal.

The Cartel Decree of 1941 attempted to change the 1935 act, as it was felt that a number of entrepreneurial agreements were contrary to the public interest. In the main, the agreements prohibited dealt with exclusive dealing and price regulation.[42] The Cartel Decree was given added legal support with the passing of the Business Agreements Suspension Act, which gave government power to suspend cartels operating contrary to public interests.

The main features of the Business Agreements Suspension Act were incorporated into the Economic Competition Act of 1956. This act attempted to control dominant market positions and to regulate competition by preventing acts of unfair practices throughout the economy.

Forms of dominant market positions operating against the public interest included the following:

Coercive action against entrepreneurs by firms, including boycotts;
Obligation to deliver;
Price controls;
Stipulation of conditions for delivery and payment.[43]

This act was amended in 1958, but the main provisions outlined have been kept. However, the problems of market size and the minimum efficiency level of a plant have been a major concern of economic analysis of competition policy for some time now. Given the relatively small size of the

Dutch market, forms of industrial combinations are encouraged when they are likely to lead to favorable results. Economies of scale, technological considerations, and international competition can in principle be advanced as reasons for favoring such an attitude.

In terms of activities of transnational corporations originating from the Netherlands, the Economic Competition Act entitled exemption "as to any regulation of competition not affecting competition in the Netherlands."[44] In other words, this would apply to overseas commercial activities of such corporations.

Japan

A similar tradition for the noncontrol of transnational corporations seems to exist in the case of Japan.[45] Before World War II, the government played an active role in promoting big business, including large-scale combines called *Zaibatsus*. The Key Industries Control Act of 1931 actively encouraged cartel activity. The procartel policy was changed in 1947 by an act relating to prohibition of private monopoly and maintenance of fair trade. The purpose of this act was made clear in Section 1, which states:

> By eliminating unreasonable restraint of production, sale, price, technology, and others through combinations, agreements, etc., and all other undue restriction of business activities, [the act] aims to promote free and fair competition, to stimulate the initiative of entrepreneurs, to encourage the business activities of entrepreneurs, to heighten the level of employment, of people's real incomes, and thereby to promote the democratic and wholesale development of the national economy.[46]

The law also attempted to deal with prohibitive international agreements involving Japanese enterprises, but this was later relaxed.

In 1948 the Trade Associations Act was passed. This act limited restrictive business practices in trade association activities.

In 1949, a process of restriction relaxation began in an effort to stimulate economic activity as part of postwar economic reconstruction. For example, control was removed over interlocking directorates and stockholding. Similar provisions were made as to international contracts and mergers. In 1953 further relaxations occurred. For example, depression cartels and rationalization cartels were allowed under special conditions. In 1952 the Export Trading Act, subsequently changed to the Export Import Trading Act, exempted control of Japanese business activity insofar as it relates to overseas trade. In the main, this exemption would seem to apply to activities of Japanese transnational corporations, including Zaibatsus trading houses, that, as we saw earlier, dominate import and export trade. Further, there are no special provisions for regulating activities of Japanese transnational corporations in production abroad.

While we have concentrated only on a group of developed countries, one study has argued that the problem of lack of control over operations of transnational corporations is usually applicable to most developed countries.[47]

European Economic Community

It is necessary to offer some comments on attempts to control restrictive business practices within the EEC. Essentially these attempts aim at setting a code of business conduct for enterprises operating in the regional market of the community. EEC members such as the United Kingdom, Germany, France, the Netherlands (as we saw earlier), as well as Italy, Belgium, and others, have legislation for controlling restrictive business practices. However, such legislation is often designed to safeguard national interests. The Treaty of Rome legislation, on the other hand, is geared to serve the wider competitive interests of the Common Market as a whole.[48] The provisions cover EEC transnational corporations operating within the Common Market, as well as other transnational corporations, such as Japanese and American firms operating therein. For example, measures to control restrictive business practices have been applied to twenty-five cases involving transnational corporations.[49] These were either headquartered in the community or were operating there through subsidiaries.

Article 85 of the treaty deals with restrictive business practices that arise as a result of collusive and other agreements between firms, and Article 86 is concerned with the abuse of dominant market power by firms.[50] For example, Article 85 prohibits "any agreement between enterprises, any decision by associations of enterprises, and any concerted practice which is likely to affect trade between member states and which have as its object or result the prevention, restriction, or distribution of competition within the Common Market."[51] These include the following:

Price fixing or any other trading condition;
Limitation or control of production, markets, technical development, or investment;
Market sharing or sharing of sources of supply;
Differential treatment that brings about competitive disadvantages;

Tied purchases that by their nature or commercial usage have no connection with the subject of such contract.

Article 86 meanwhile lists the following prohibited restrictive business practices, which relate to market practices by dominant firms:

The direct or indirect imposition of any inequitable purchase or selling prices or of any other inequitable trading conditions;
The limitation of production, markets, or technical development to the prejudice of consumers;
The application to parties to transactions of unequal terms in respect to equivalent supplies, thereby placing them at a competitive disadvantage;
The subjecting of the conclusion of a contract to a party's acceptance of additional supplies that, either by their nature or according to commercial usage, have no connection with the subject of such contract.[52]

Articles 85 and 86 represent a courageous attempt by the EEC to ensure that the competitive process is at work outside national boundaries of individual member states. However, it should be noted that control of restrictive business practices by the EEC does not apply to forms of economic transactions affecting third countries in general and developing countries in particular. For instance, under Articles 85 and 86 cartels that fix prices or quantities of goods that are imported into the EEC "may be prohibited."[53] However, if the trade or competition within the EEC is not affected, the import cartel may be allowed to operate. The same applies to export cartels.[54] In a recent study, we showed that a number of restrictive business practices involving EEC transnational corporations are allowed to exist in a large number of developing countries.[55] This is true even though such practices are declared illegal within the EEC itself.

Let us summarize. We saw the existence of legislative attempts by the countries under review to control restrictive business practices of various sorts. In many instances, there has been the strengthening of national laws to this end. A major shortcoming of these laws, however, seems to be the inadequate treatment accorded to activities of national enterprises when they operate internationally.[56] In the case of the EEC, for example, overseas activities of transnational corporations may be subjected to regulation, but this does not apply if such corporations' activities do not directly affect trade and competition within the EEC. A parallel situation exists for individual developed countries. However, most developed countries have laws that may take into account operations of foreign transnational corporations operating within their national boundaries. For example, national restrictive business practices laws will automatically embrace these corporations. As we will shortly see, this situation is not the same for developing countries.

This situation has led researchers to argue for international measures for the control of restrictive business practices not covered by national laws and, in particular, those practices arising from transnational corporations.[57] Meanwhile, it is of interest to evaluate the effectiveness of restrictive business practices legislation in terms of growing industrial concentration, which, as we saw earlier, scant evidence suggests is the case.

Forms of gross market imperfection, as we saw, do potentially give rise to forms of restrictive business practices. Restrictive business practices also theoretically could lead to undesirable social and economic consequences. Thus, the argument could be made that the laws, if they are effective, should come to terms with this structure of markets leading to possible abuse. It should be noted, however, that some countries may approach dominant market positions through a market-conduct approach rather than looking at the market structure as such.[58] In other words, they allow concentrations to take place or to continue while at the same time ensuring, through competition policy, that these concentrations do not operate against the public interest.

LEGISLATION IN DEVELOPING COUNTRIES

Under optimistic assumptions—namely, if developing countries have adequate restrictive business practices legislation to control activities of transnational corporations—the problem would prima facie cease to be one of major concern. The actual situation, however, gives reason for some pessimism. A recent survey of countries with restrictive business practices legislation shows that only very few developing countries had such.[59] In countries with such legislation, variations occur in terms of recency, scope, and detail of laws. The effectiveness of such legislation is, however, subject to serious doubts in a large number of these cases.[60] A recent UN resolution, in recognition of the problem, indicated that "urgent consideration should be given to the formulation of a model law for the control of restrictive business practices in developing countries."[61] Further, UNCTAD's work in the area of assisting the formulation of laws for controlling restrictive business practices has been described as "pioneering."[62] This not only attests to a major policy-gap problem; it also remains an open question both as to what the "model law" should entail and what it is expected to achieve.

Among developing countries that have legislation for the control of restrictive business practices are Malaysia, India, Pakistan, and some countries in Latin America. Let us look briefly at some of the available legislation in developing countries.

Caribbean Community

Article 30 of the Treaty Establishing the Caribbean Community recognized the following restrictive business practices to be incompatible with the development objectives of member states:

> Agreements between enterprises, decisions by associations of enterprises, and concerted practices between enterprises that have as their object or result the prevention, restriction, or distortion of competition within the Common Market;
> Actions by which one or more enterprises take unfair advantage of a dominant position within the Common Market or a substantial part of it.[63]

The treaty also makes mention of the need to consider additional provisions for the effective control of restrictive business practices. In this light, the Common Market is expected to conduct reviews in the following areas:

> Specification of restrictive business practices or dominant enterprises with which the council should be concerned;
> Methods of securing information about restrictive business practices or dominant enterprises;
> Investigation procedures.[64]

So far, machinery for regulating restrictive business practices has not yet been established in the Secretariat of the Common Market. Also, while the treaty calls on member states to introduce uniform legislation for the control of restrictive business practices, such legislation has yet to be implemented at the time of writing.[65] In a sense, therefore, the interest in the Common Market in controlling restrictive business practices is only at the purely formal stage.

India

The Monopolies and Restrictive Trade Practices Act of 1969 in India attempts to ensure "that the operation of the economic system does not result in the concentration of economic power to the common detriment, for the control of monopolies, for the prohibition of monopolistic and restrictive trade practices. . . ."[66] These include predatory pricing, restriction in the distribution or supply of goods, and the limitation of technical development. The law draws a distinction between dominant enterprises—namely, those having at least 30 percent of the domestic market share—and monopolistic ones—those that control not less than 50 percent of the market share. The law applies to most sectors of the economy, including the public sector and banking and finance.[67] A Monopolies and Restrictive Business Practices agency has been set up to probe cases of unfair practices.

Pakistan

In 1970 a Monopolies and Restrictive Trade Practices Ordinance was announced in Pakistan. Its sole objective is "to provide for measures against undue concentration of economic power, growth of unreasonable monopoly power, and unreasonable restrictive trade practices."[68] The underlying rationale for this is that these elements "are injurious to economic well-being, growth, and development in Pakistan."[69] Unreasonable monopoly power is defined under this act as constituting at least 20 percent of the local market share. The act addresses itself mainly to the following practices:

Market-sharing arrangements;
Limitation of output;
Limitation of technical development;
Use of boycott;
Resale price maintenance.

In the cases of Pakistan, India, and the Caribbean community, existing restrictive business practices laws make no special reference to transnational corporations. The approach is therefore general in nature. This might be considered as a weakness in the existing approaches by these countries to control such practices, given the special problem that transnational corporations pose to the development of such countries. Alternately, it could be argued that room for discretion exists in the application of these general laws to make allowance for this weakness. Also, it could be contended that a general approach could serve as a useful preliminary to more specific legal policy that takes into account the role of transnational corporations. Be that as it may, it should be noted that a number of developing countries, for example, following a type of infant-industry argument familiar to development economies have been arguing for preferential treatment to be given to domestic enterprises in a number of areas in international economic affairs.[70] Often, too, the rationale for this treatment is advanced in terms of reducing dependency on transnational enterprises and the like by actively encouraging "countervailing" enterprises in developing countries themselves.[71] The merits and demerits of this do not concern us here.

Malaysia

In a number of other cases, however, legislation in developing countries does make specific reference to transnational corporations. One example is the Malaysian approach. The Guidelines for the Regulation of Acquisition of Assets, Mergers, and Takeovers of 1974 draws attention to the substantial foreign ownership of the country's economic activities.[72] The guidelines accordingly stipulate that attempts by foreign firms to increase market control will be discouraged if positive contribution to economic development in Malaysia is not envisaged. Activities of transnational corporations in "new areas," such as exports of manufactured goods and marketing, will, however, be encouraged. On the whole, the guidelines seek to increase the share of national firms in economic activity in Malaysia.

Latin America

In a comprehensive study on restrictive business practices legislation in Latin America, Eduardo White showed that in a number of countries, such as Argentina, Brazil, Chile, Colombia, and Mexico, a distinction is usually made between "domestic" market power and "imported" market power —the latter arising in the context of international economic activity.[73] Special approaches are being developed for the control of dominant market power and practices of transnational corporations, especially in the area of transfer pricing and territorial market-allocation arrangements. In terms of transfer pricing, the prevailing approach, according to the study, includes the enforcement of arms-length (free-market) prices for intracorporate transactions; the requirement that the basis for pricing decisions be given in the event of difficulties in evaluating arms-length prices; and the disclosure of information on purchases, sales, and profits.[74] This includes royalties and intracorporate loans. In most of the countries, royalty payments between parents and subsidiaries are reportedly prohibited on the grounds that the corporation is regarded as a single legal entity and is not capable of charging itself for royalties.[75]

In Argentina, interest payments on company loans are regarded as dividend remittances, and in the Andean Group of countries, the rates of interest that can be charged on intracorporate loans are tightly controlled.[76] In addition, the Andean Group places strong emphasis on the elimination of restrictive business practices of transnational corporations as they affect the transfer of technology.[77]

In the area of territorial market-allocation arrangements, most of the Latin American countries pay attention to those relating to the restriction of exports.[78] In this light, minimum export levels for transnationals are established in Argentina, Brazil, Colombia, and Mexico.[79]

Even so, there remains the problem of evaluating the efforts of developing countries to control restrictive business practices of transnational corporations. Remember that most developing countries are short of key resources. As a result, the attraction of foreign capital forms a key feature in their national development policies. Because of this and because laws for controlling restrictive business practices are not uniform in developing countries, the inevitable risk is that if a country makes too strong a demand for control, it is likely to "kill the goose that lays the golden egg." If one assumes, optimistically, that the "general-rule" cases of countries such as India and Pakistan do provide enough flexibility for controlling practices of transnational corporations, the problem is by no means fully resolved.

On balance, in countries having both general and specific laws, evidence seems to suggest that these laws have failed to be fully effective in controlling market structures and the growth of economic power as they affect such corporations.[80] However, some measure of success has been reported in some countries in the area of the protection of consumer interests as they relate to price increases.[81] For example, in Latin America one of the principal difficulties is with the enforcement of national laws. Lack of autonomy of competent authorities, inadequate resources to organize efficient organs of control, and lack of specificity of the laws have been some of the reasons attributed to this difficulty.[82] Another reason lies in what might be called "the gestation period." Most experts seem to believe that effective control of restrictive business practices entails a lengthy period, running into decades. The experience of developed countries seems to confirm this somewhat.

Given the gravity of the situation then, it is not surprising that international efforts are now being actively geared at offering technical assistance to developing countries in the area of legislation for the control of restrictive business practices.[83] This task can, in many respects, be regarded as enormous given (1) limited resources at the international level that seem to exist in the field, and (2) the apparent lack of a political will in a large number of developing countries to devise adequate institutional measures. The latter is sometimes due to the lack of awareness of the problem by policymakers.

4 TRANSNATIONAL CORPORATIONS AND DEVELOPING COUNTRIES

Transnational corporations have become an important feature in the world economy. Their activities cover most sectors of economic importance —agriculture, mining, manufacturing, marketing and distribution, and banking and finance. In 1971, the value added of the top ten transnational corporations was in excess of U.S. $3 billion, which was more than the gross domestic product of eighty developing countries.[1] At the same time, the value added of transnational corporations as a group was estimated at U.S. $500 billion, or 20 percent of the world's national product, if centrally planned economies were excluded.[2]

Another index sometimes used as a measure of the importance of transnational corporations is international production, which is defined as production subject to foreign control or decisions and is measured by the sales of foreign affiliates of such corporations. In 1971, international production had surpassed trade as the main vehicle of international economic exchange. For example, according to UN estimates, international production was U.S. $330 billion, while total exports of all market economies were U.S. $310 billion.[3] (See Table 4.1.)

Data show that the total estimated world stock of foreign direct investment was U.S. $165 billion in 1971. Most of this was owned by transna-

47

Table 4.1.   Market Economies: International Production and Exports, 1971
(in million of dollars)

Country[a]	Stock of Foreign Direct Investment of Transnationals (book value)	Estimated International Production[b]	Exports	International Production as Percentage of Exports
United States	86,000	172,000	43,492	395.5
United Kingdom	24,020	48,000	22,367	214.6
France	9,540	19,100	20,420	93.5
Federal Republic of Germany	7,270	14,600	39,040	37.4
Switzerland	6,760	13,500	5,728	235.7
Canada	5,930	11,900	17,582	67.7
Japan	4,480	9,000	24,019	37.5
The Netherlands	3,580	7,200	13,927	51.7
Sweden	3,450	6,900	7,465	92.4
Italy	3,350	6,700	15,111	44.3
Belgium	3,250	6,500	12,392	52.4
Australia	610	1,200	5,070	23.7
Portugal	320	600	1,052	57.0
Denmark	310	600	3,685	16.3
Norway	90	200	2,563	7.8
Austria	40	100	3,169	3.2
Total DAC	159,000	318,100	237,082	133.7
Total other[c]	6,000	12,000	74,818	16.0
Total market economies	165,000	330,100	311,900	105.8

Source: Centre for Development Planning, Projections and Policies of the Department of Economic and Social Affairs of the UN Secretariat, based on Table 5; and *Monthly Bulletin of Statistics* 27 (UN publication, April 1973).

[a]Countries are listed in descending order of book value of foreign direct investment.

[b]Estimated international production equals the book value of foreign direct investment multiplied by the factor 2.0. The estimate of this factor was derived as follows: The ratio of foreign sales to book value of foreign direct investment has been estimated from 1970 U.S. data on gross sales of majority-owned foreign affiliates and book value of U.S. foreign direct investment. Gross sales of majority-owned foreign affiliates (approximately $157 billion) include transactions between foreign affiliates and parent corporations (approximately $20.3 billion) and interforeign affiliate sales (approximately $28.1 billion), which together account for about 30 percent of gross foreign affiliate sales.

[c]Non-DAC countries, including developing countries.

tional corporations. Four developed countries—the United States, France, Germany, and the United Kingdom—accounted for 80 percent of this stock.[4] More than half of it was owned by the United States (see Table 4.1). While changes in the country-ownership characteristics of transnational corporations have certainly taken place over the years, evidence does point to the fact that the relative significance of these four countries in overseas investment has been basically unaltered or changed just slightly.

Further, data on the growth of transnational corporations call for comment. Between 1950 and 1966 the size of affiliates of U.S. transnationals more than trebled—from 7,417 to 23,282. In the case of EEC transnationals, the increase was threefold; a fourfold increase was recorded for Japan.[5] Between 1960 and 1971, the book value of U.S. direct overseas investment increased from U.S. $33 billion to U.S. $86 billion, and the United King-

Table 4.2. Selected Developed Market Economies: Stock of Foreign Direct Investment, 1960–1971 (in millions of dollars and percentage)

Year	Japan	Federal Republic of Germany	United Kingdom	United States
Book Value (millions of dollars)				
1960	289.0	758.1	11,988.2	32,765
1961	453.8	968.7[a]	12,912.1	34,664
1962	535.2	1,239.6	13,649.1	37,149
1963	679.2	1,527.3	14,646.2	40,686
1964	799.5	1,811.7	16,415.6	44,386
1965	956.2	2,076.1	16,796.5	49,328
1966	1,183.2	2,513.2	17,531.4	54,711
1967	1,458.1	3,015.0	17,521.1[a]	59,486
1968	2,015.3	3,587.0	18,478.8	64,983
1969	2,682.9	4,774.5[a]	20,043.2	71,016
1970	3,596.3	5,774.5	21,390.5	78,090
1971	4,480.0[a]	7,276.9[a]	24,019.0[a]	86,001
Average Annual Rate of Growth (percentage)				
1960–1965	27.0	22.3	7.0	8.5
1965–1971	29.4	23.2	6.1	9.7
1960–1971	28.3	22.8	6.5	9.2

Source: Centre for Development Planning, Projections and Policies of the Department of Economic and Social Affairs of the UN Secretariat, as extracted from *Multinational Corporations in World Development* (New York, 1973).
[a]Exchange rate change.

dom's grew from U.S. $12 billion to U.S. $24 billion. In Japan, the increase was fifteenfold—from U.S. $300 million to U.S. $4.5 billion. For Germany, it increased almost tenfold—to U.S. $7.3 billion. At the same time, statistics show the average annual rate of growth in these investments to be as follows: 28.3 percent, Japan; 22.8 percent, Germany; 6.5 percent, United Kingdom; 9.2 percent, United States. The respective corporate growth rates have been far more impressive than the average real economic growth rates in each of these countries. Table 4.2 gives a breakdown of the data just cited.

INVESTMENT THEORY, INTERNATIONAL INVESTMENT, AND TRANSNATIONALS

Investment theory refined by Keynes posits that the inducement to invest is a function of the rate of interest and the marginal efficiency of capital.[6] The latter is in fact the expected yield of the investment project that Keynes defined as "being equal to that rate of discount which would make the present value of the series of annuities given by the returns expected from the capital asset during its life just equal to its supply price."[7] The supply price of an asset, sometimes called its *replacement cost,* is basically the price that the entrepreneur pays to acquire a capital asset, say, a plant. As to the rate of interest, an investor who has liquid resources available for investment usually discovers that he has an alternative to investing his money in new capital equipment. For example, he can earn interest by putting his money into bonds instead of taking the risk in investing in a factory and hoping that it will be a success. It follows that investment will be undertaken only if the investor expects to earn money that is at least equal to the rate of interest or the opportunity cost. Conversely, if we assume that the businessperson must finance the proposed project by using debentures, it is also clear that the expected yield of the project must never fall below the interest rate; otherwise, it will cease to be profitable.

Figure 4.1 depicts this situation simplistically. The marginal efficiency of capital (MEC) falls as more investment is undertaken in a particular asset. The reason is twofold. The first applies to the law of diminishing returns known to us and needs no further elaboration. The second is that the supply price of the asset will tend to increase in the short run in the industry making the asset and if we assume full capacity utilization in the asset-producing sector. Rising supply costs need not necessarily be the case in the long run. If we now assume a fall in interest rate from 1 to $1''$ on the given MEC schedule, we can invest larger amounts—say, from $0M$ to $0M''$.

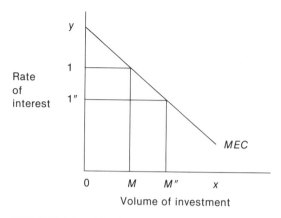

FIGURE 4.1.　Marginal Efficiency of Capital

This theory, however, is not very useful in analyzing the international investment behavior of transnational corporations. In the case of domestic investment, Hall and Hitch have long ago shown that it does not take one very far.[8] There are two basic problems with the theory. One is that it is very static, and the other is that it does not tell us much about how strategic considerations affect investment decisions in the real world. The theory follows a somewhat profit-maximizing assumption under which profits are seen as the sole objective of the firm. In a different connection, we saw in Chapter 1 that there has been some criticism of this. A number of alternative theories with varying levels of plausibility have been put forward. Papandreou, Scitovsky, Williamson, and others have suggested that managers seek to maximize utility instead of only profits.[9] This utility is a function of internal and external demands of the firm. Roberts, McGuire et al., and Baumol have argued that firms seek to maximize sales rather than profits.[10] This, it is reasoned, is a result of the separation of ownership from control and the link between sales and profits. Concepts of output maximization have been explored by Ames and Kafoglis.[11] Averch and Johnson have alternatively suggested that constrained output and profit maximization are the main considerations underlying the behavior of firms.[12] Simon and others, as we saw earlier, have suggested that a number of behavioral considerations feature as the main objectives of the firm.

Specifically, in terms of investment decisions by transnational enterprises—namely, foreign direct investment—empirical investigations have found the following considerations to be relevant: the search for raw materials as part of the production strategy, especially in the case of enterprises engaged in agriculture and mining;[13] cost-reducing considerations, for example, production and transport costs and tariffs;[14] locational and marketing strategies;[15] nonprice factors, such as antitrust legislation, prevailing political climate (including prospects to repatriate profits), and servicing of foreign markets;[16] defensive strategies relating to the risk of loss of markets or sources of supply;[17] product differentiation and sellers' concentration;[18] changing technological ascendancy; and the unique-assets theory, such as the product-cycle theory, among others.[19]

Thus, the existing literature largely assumes that foreign direct investment by transnationals is a function of goods and factor market imperfections. Basically, the foreign investor requires some source of advantage that can be contained and exploited—namely, some form of monopoly rent. International production and limiting access by local firms to markets are means through which monopoly rent can be augmented and profits correspondingly increased.

TRANSNATIONAL CORPORATIONS AS DOMINANT-FIRM TYPES

Models of oligopoly behavior, such as those of Cournot, Von Stackelberg, and others, discussed earlier, can be extended in principle to apply to activities of transnational firms in developing countries—for example, activities relating to forms of price collusion and entry-forestalling techniques. Most of these models, it may be recalled, point to attempts by firms, jointly or singly, to restrict competition. These models were found to be largely static. However, combining dynamic aspects of oligopolistic competition as it relates to transnational firms can bring one closer to home.[20]

In this connection, the product-cycle theory just cited informs us that foreign direct investment by transnationals is often undertaken as a defensive strategy to maintain already established market positions.[21] The idea here is to prevent potential competitors from displacing original exporters of a particular good in a given market. In this connection, Vaitsos has argued that foreign direct investment retards the competitive process and is often directed toward the preservation of monopoly positions overseas.[22] Other investigators, such as Vernon, have developed the concept of entropy—namely, the process by which firms lose their inner energy—to explain attempts by transnationals to extend market-dominating or oligopolistic strategies beyond domestic markets.[23] The argument is that "if leaders have enjoyed an especially high price or a special degree of stability because buyers think that their products are unique, the entry of new firms is seen as threatening the premium or weakening the stability that the leaders enjoyed."[24] The argument continues that in any product line that faces the prospect of entry of new firms, the established leaders tend to see themselves threatened. Thus, " . . . the investment decisions of multinational enterprises in developing countries have approached conditioned reflexes, instinctive reactions calculated to fend off some threatened or matched initiative by a rival firm."[25] A similar position has been advanced by Knickerbocker in terms of explaining the growth and spread of transnational firms internationally.[26]

Other writers have stressed the role of acquisitions and mergers as a means of strengthening the market power of transnationals overseas[27]—for example, in the manufacturing sector of a large number of developing countries.[28]

A study has argued that restrictive business practices' effects of mergers involving transnationals reveal themselves largely in the degree of concentration and barriers to entry that follow.[29] Both of these factors in turn enable firms to exercise market power in terms of fixing prices and output. However, it remains true that mergers may facilitate technical economies of scale, among other things. Edwards has further argued that conglomerate mergers have an ability to "rechannel funds and spread risks, subsidize one activity from the proceeds of another, enjoy the benefits of joint revenues, spread large lump-sum costs over multiple products, undertake vertical integration, get bargaining advantages to do so and to resort to reciprocity."[30] Thus, it can be argued that forms of conglomerate mergers tend to give some firms special competitive advantages over rivals.

Caves has reminded us that overseas investments of the vertical, horizontal, or conglomerate types are features of attempts by transnational firms to foster market control overseas.[31] In terms of vertical investments, the argument is that they are prompted by two main considerations; the first concerns the avoidance of oligopolistic uncertainty, and the other arises from the need to erect barriers to entry. According to this position, "By controlling their input sources, the existing firm may secure structural barriers to the entry of new competition. If main supply sources are tied up through vertical integration, a new entrant to the processing industry must endure the extra costs and uncertainty of finding and developing his own sources of raw materials. The going firm can enjoy higher-than-competitive profit rates without attracting new rivals. . . ."[32] The strategic importance of this point is especially relevant to natural resource–based transnationals.[33]

Further, evidence suggests the increasing involvement of transnational corporations in marketing and distribution outlets in developing countries. Often the motive here is "to maximize quasirents on their technological discoveries and differentiated products."[34] Hymer and Rowthorn meanwhile have looked at foreign direct investment by transnationals as a form of interpenetration "by which the interests of small firms in each country are sacrificed to the interest of big firms in other countries."[35]

A number of empirical studies have documented the presence of oligopolistic markets in which transnational corporations operate. According to Vernon, transnationals with annual sales of less than U.S. $100 million can be safely ignored because of their relative unimportance.[36] Evidence of large size is further supported by a UN study on transnationals.[37] The study shows that in 1971 each of the four largest transnationals had annual sales volumes of more than U.S. $10 billion and that more than two hundred transnationals exceeded the U.S. $1 billion mark.[38] Most of these ranked among the largest firms in the world and had affiliates in more than twenty countries. We have already noted the distinction between firm size and market structure. However, evidence, albeit incomplete, seems to suggest that in the case of transnationals large size is often associated with oligopolistic type of markets both in the home country and in host ones.[39] Over three thousand transnational corporations that were not considered large scale were reported to have been in existence in 1971, but their overall activity, as already noted, was reported as not very important.[40] It should be noted, however, that it is possible that such "internationally small" transnationals may also occupy positions of dominant market power in some developing countries. This is especially true where small domestic markets prevail, acute shortages of local entrepreneurs exist, or special production rights are conferred on an overseas firm to encourage investment of some sort or another.

On balance, the size of transnational corporations has led some economists to regard them as a threat to the national sovereignty of developing countries.[41] This is often so because the size of such enterprises confers upon them certain strategic importance in the sectors in which they operate in such countries. We already noted the relationship between some transnationals and the gross domestic product of a large number of developing countries.

A UN study provides further evidence of the fact that the typical market in which transnationals operate is dominated by a few buyers or sellers. The markets are said to be characterized by the importance of "new technologies, or of special skills, or of product differentiation and heavy advertising which sustains or reinforces their oligopolistic nature."[42]

In a study on the activities of transnational corporations as they affect developing countries, UNCTAD has argued that such corporations, as a result of their dominant market power, often command oligopolistic and monopolistic market positions in relation to the production and marketing of goods imported and exported by developing countries.[43]

Another crude guide of dominant-type firms operating transnationally may be found in the following figures relating to the high degree of concentration in foreign direct investment. These figures deal with what might be called "the export of foreign direct investment" by parent countries of transnationals. In the case of the United States, 250–300 firms accounted for 70 percent of the grand total in 1971. At the same time, in the United Kingdom 165 firms accounted for 80 percent, and in Germany 82 firms accounted for 70 percent, with the largest 9 controlling 37 percent.[44] Similar concentration patterns appear to exist for France and the Netherlands. In the case of Japan, although many relatively small-sized firms are active in foreign investment pursuits, the leading Japanese trading houses play an important direct and indirect role in overseas production. It will be recalled that these trading houses play an important role in Japanese foreign trade. Some evidence exists of growing concentrations of transnational corporations in other countries, notably France, Germany, the United States, and the United Kingdom, in terms of marketing and distribution of goods internationally.[45] This situation has now led to the concept of transnational marketing corporations found, for example, in most of UNCTAD's recent work on transnational corporations and trade of manufactured goods.

Let us turn to the export structure of developed countries since the developing countries obtain the bulk of their industrial goods from this source. Evidence suggests that most of these goods are found in sectors in which transnational corporations operate. Accordingly, transnationals are sometimes reported to command as much as 80 percent of the export market share in some sectors.[46] Technology exported from developed countries is similarly dominated by transnational firms. We return to this shortly.

We mentioned earlier the importance of oligopolistic forces in host countries. Let us look at the situation more closely. Little hard research has been conducted on the market structures in developing countries in which transnational corporations are found. In some cases, researchers tend to assume, somewhat intuitively, that market dominance in a developing country will automatically arise as a result of the dominant position of a particular transnational corporation in a parent country. Sometimes generalization is based on a particular experience. However, the experiences of one country may also be inapplicable to others; the experiences of one sector need not necessarily receive confirmation in other sectors. However, empirical findings do exist that seem to bear testimony to the fact that transnational corporations tend to operate in highly concentrated markets in some developing countries. The findings of these studies confirm to some extent the hypothesis that oligopolistic market structures characterize the activities of transnational corporations in the production of goods and services overseas.

Meller, in a study on concentration in Latin America, has found that "there exists a similar pattern of industrial concentration in Latin America. . . . Industries with the highest levels of concentration are tobacco, rubber, basic metals, and paper. Latin American countries which have smaller market size have systematically higher levels of concentration than others."[47] Newfarmer and Mueller have found oligopolistic market forces in existence in Mexico and Brazil.[48] In Argentina, Sourrouille has found that between 1970 and 1973 more than two-thirds of foreign industrial produce stemmed from subgroups in which they dominated over 75 percent of the market, and 75 percent came from subgroups in which they dominated over 50 percent of the market.[49] Similar evidence is revealed for Central America by Willmore.[50] Findings to this effect are also confirmed in the Caribbean and parts of Africa in terms of both manufacturing and primary-sector activities.[51] In a study on plantations, Beckford has found a similar pattern in a number of developing countries in Asia, the Caribbean, Latin America, and Africa.[52] In the case of mining in developing countries, a similar pattern appears to exist. In many cases, governments now operate in partnership with transnational corporations. The traditional pattern, however, is one of private control by transnationals—for example, of bauxite in Jamaica and Guyana and copper in Chile and Zambia.

Further, transnational banks are known to exert an important influence in the banking sector of many developing economies in the Caribbean and parts of Africa, Asia, and Latin America.[53] This evidence shows attempts to change banking structures dominated by transnational corporations in a number of developing countries. Often, however, such banks continue to play a relatively important role even though their absolute market share may have been eroded.[54]

A number of sectoral studies on pharmaceutical, electrical, and automobile industries, among others, also point to evidence that transnationals operate in oligopolistic market structures in developing countries.[55] The situation concerning the dominant market power of transnational corporations in developing countries has led Lall to argue that "the fact that industrial concentration has tended to increase in developed countries and that the growth of transnational corporations has taken place mainly in sectors characterized by growing oligopoly may suggest that transnational corporations have actually caused a rise in the concentration in sectors in which they are active."[56]

In Chapter, 1 we discussed the problems that may arise as a result of market structures of the type we have identified in this section. Before we attempt to relate this specifically to problems of development, we must offer a survey of available data on activities of transnational corporations as they affect developing countries.

ACTIVITIES OF TRANSNATIONAL CORPORATIONS AND DEVELOPING COUNTRIES

Estimates for 1971 show that out of the total foreign direct investment of U.S. $165 billion (mentioned earlier), approximately U.S. $57 billion, or 30 percent, was invested in developing countries.[57] According to the United Nations, the presence of transnational corporations in developing countries is of greater relative significance to such countries than to developed ones.[58] The reasons for this are not hard to find. First, the aggregated gross domestic product of developing countries is considerably lower than that of developed countries. Further, capital and technology are in extremely short supply in developing countries. Transnational corporations tend to be the main suppliers of these items. Also, since developing countries are anxious to accelerate their industrial development, clearly transnational corporations will have to be relied upon in the foreseeable future to be an agent of development. How that move is guided is another matter and does not presently concern us.

Historically, transnational corporations were primarily induced to invest in developing countries in a drive to secure raw materials—in agriculture and mining—for their vertically integrated production structures. The experiences of Unilever, Booker McConnell, and Tate and Lyle, three of the oldest agriculturally based transnational corporations, are cases in point. Their activities were located mainly in Africa and the Caribbean. In the main, primary agriculture was used as a basis for supplying inputs for agroindustrial processing in metropolitan countries. In many cases, colonies with a comparative advantage in raw materials served as convenient networks for the supply of such materials to international enterprises. The same holds for mining—for example, of bauxite, copper, zinc, cobalt—in parts of Africa and the Caribbean. Limited processing of such materials took place locally, while most processing activity took place overseas where the parent company was headquartered. Over the years, governments in developing countries have moved to change the pattern of agriculture specialization and have consequently taken greater control over the operations of transnational corporations in the area. Table 4.3 shows, for example, that toward 1970 only 6.2 percent of foreign direct investment was in agriculture. Other factors have certainly contributed to the relative decline of agriculture, such as the growing importance of other sectors (for instance,

Table 4.3. Foreign Direct Investment, by Sector and Developing Region, End 1967

Sector[a]	Total (millions of dollars)	Share in Total Stock of DAC Countries (percentage)	Distribution among Developing Regions (percentage)			
			Africa	Western Hemisphere[b]	Middle East	Asia
Petroleum	10,962	33.1	23.1	40.9	25.3	10.1
Manufacturing	9,627	29.1	12.8	69.1	2.0	16.1
Mining and smelting	3,554	10.7	36.0	56.7	0.2	7.1
Trade	2,601	7.8	15.3	64.1	1.2	19.4
Agriculture	2,046	6.2	24.3	29.7	0.1	45.9
Public utilities	1,570	4.7	4.2	87.3	0.7	7.8
Transport	676	2.0	32.8	54.4	2.7	10.1
Banking	588	1.8	23.9	48.7	4.7	22.7
Tourism	448	1.4	9.8	57.9	4.0	28.3
Other	1,063	3.2	10.4	69.2	2.2	18.2
Total	33,135	100.0	19.9	55.6	9.4	15.1

Source: Centre for Development Planning, Projections and Policies of the Department of Economic and Social Affairs of the UN Secretariat, based on OECD, Stock of Private Direct Investments by DAC Countries in Developing Countries, End 1967 (Paris, 1972).
[a]Sectors are arranged in descending order of value of stock of direct private investment in developing regions.
[b]Latin America and the Caribbean.

manufacturing and the tertiary sector), that has accompanied the increase in world real incomes over the past few decades. We saw previously that income elasticity or demand for many agricultural products does not generally compare favorably to manufactured products.

In the case of mining (excluding petroleum), a similar policy of government intervention has in part contributed to the relative decline of transnationals in this sector over the years. For example, a recent study by the EEC showed that EEC transnational corporations had been disinvesting in the mining sector of developing countries as a whole.[59] The study noted that greater control by Third World governments over their natural resources was the prime reason for the changing attitude by EEC transnationals toward overseas investment in mining. As Table 4.3 shows, mining occupied about 11 percent or U.S. $3.5 billion in the total share of overseas investment in developing countries by transnationals in 1967. In the meantime, petroleum continues to be a relatively important sector for transnational corporations. Toward the end of 1960, about 33 percent of total foreign direct investment by transnationals, or U.S. $11 billion, was in the petroleum sector. An evaluation of the effect of OPEC on transnational activity in petroleum is still being awaited. It must, however, be noted that most of the technology involved in petroleum extraction, exploration, and refining is controlled by transnationals connected within this sector. On the other hand, growing evidence shows that transnationals are increasing their activities in other energy-related sectors (for example, solar and tidal).

One of the fastest growing areas of transnational activity in developing countries is manufacturing. Manufacturing was virtually nonexistent in the 1940s. Estimates for 1967, for example, showed that nearly U.S. $10 billion, or 29 percent, of total foreign direct investment in developing countries was in manufacturing. (See Table 4.3.) The growth of manufacturing investment in developing countries has been partly a result of import substitution industrialization in many countries, on the one hand, and the promotion of export-processing zones, on the other. Often, incentives have been offered to transnational corporations by developing countries so as to activate both of these. We have noted, in a different context, the shortage of capital, technology, and vital skills that developing countries tend to experience—hence, the gap-filling importance of transnationals. The need to industrialize was considered urgent by many developing countries, given their undue dependency on one or two export commodities and the assumption that manufacturing activity was vital for economic development. Low price and income elasticity of demand for these commodities, to which mention has already been made, seemed to offer poor growth and employment prospects. This emphasis on manufacturing activity, however, was subjected to criticism since it was felt by some analysts that it reduced the potential for agriculture in economic development. Manufacturing growth was often associated with a decline in agricultural output. The shortage of wage goods that this decline set in train resulted in high food-import bills for many countries, thereby aggravating the balance-of-payments problems.[60]

In Latin America and other developing countries, the drive toward industrialization was further induced by the effect of World War II, which cut off supplies of manufactured goods from abroad for local consumption. It also froze export markets. Investment allowances including taxes and the repatriation of profits, the availability of cheap labor supplies, a ready domestic or foreign market including those operating under regional integration schemes,[61] and a suitable political climate are often cited as some of the main factors that have helped to induce transnationals interested in import-substitution ventures to invest in many developing countries.[62] Later, as domestic markets became saturated, attempts were made to transform the import-substitution-led industrialization into export promotion. The saturation of the home market meant that if growth in real output was to continue, new markets had to be found. Often, however, this new feature of industrialization encountered several problems, including international competitiveness of industries set up under the protective walls of tariffs.[63]

Apart from this conversion process, a number of developing countries had embarked upon export promotion as a concerted policy to begin with. More specifically, investigations reveal that an important area of manufacturing activity by transnational firms in developing countries relates to what is sometimes regarded as "new-assembly type." One type is sometimes called new labor-intensive final products for exports, which uses mainly unskilled labor-intensive techniques. A number of poor countries are said to have a comparative advantage in this "unskilled-labor" production type.[64] For example, textiles, sporting equipment, shoes, toys, and so on, would be included. The other type involves skilled labor-intensive processes and component specialization, as distinct from final products, within vertically integrated transnational firms.[65]

During the second half of the 1960s, there was a rapid emergence of export-processing activities as a leading sector in such countries as Hong Kong, Taiwan, India, Mexico, South Korea, Brazil, Argentina, Pakistan, the Philippines, Iran, Malaysia, and Singapore.[66] Data show that automobile parts are manufactured for British, American, and Japanese transnationals in the following countries: radio antennae in Taiwan; piston rings and cylinder linings in South Korea and Taiwan; automobile lamps in Mexico; braking equipment in India; and batteries and springs in Thailand. In a large number of countries, transnationals are active in the production of electrical appliances, including televisions and radios, sewing machines, calculators, office equipment, electrical machinery, power tools, machine tools and parts, motorcycles, typewriters, cameras, optical equipment, aircraft parts, telecommunications equipment, as well as chemicals, synthetic fibers, and so on.[67]

Meanwhile, some fifty-odd developing countries that are members of the Lome Convention have been demanding, as part of the economic cooperation agreement with the EEC, the increase of processing of their raw materials as part of a drive to diversify their economies. (The Lome Convention, an economic-cooperation arrangement between the European community and a group of African, Caribbean, and Pacific states, was signed in 1975.) The demand includes mineral processing as well as processing in agriculture and forestry. Hard evidence awaits the exact role of transnationals here, but one suspects that given the role of such corporations in the Lome-Group developing countries to begin with, a growing importance of transnationals in these "new agroindustrial" areas is likely.

Transnational corporations in developing countries are involved in other areas apart from those already cited. For instance, in 1967 trade took up U.S. $2.6 billion, or 8 percent of overall activity; public utilities, U.S. $1.6 billion, or about 5 percent; transport, U.S. $676 million, or 2 percent; banking, U.S. $588 million, or 1.8 percent; and tourism, U.S. $448 million, or 1.4 percent, as Table 4.3 shows. These, however, are averages.

In the case of petroleum, nearly 90 percent of foreign direct investment in the Middle East was in this sector. In Asia it was 22 percent, and in Africa 39 percent. In some African countries, such as Nigeria and Gabon, the amount was found to be much higher than the continental average. In the case of manufacturing, although the overall share of transnational corporation activities in developing countries was 29 percent, in Africa it was 19 percent, or U.S. $1.2 billion; in Asia it was 31 percent, or U.S. $1.5 billion; and in Latin America and the Caribbean, it was the highest—36 percent, or U.S. $6.7 billion. Likewise in mining and smelting, the share was highest in Africa—19.4 percent, or U.S. $1.3 billion; second highest in Latin America and the Caribbean—11 percent, or U.S. $2 billion; and lowest in the Middle East, where it was less than 1 percent. In the case of agriculture, the highest share of foreign direct investment through transnationals was recorded in Asia—19 percent, or U.S. $939 million—with the lowest share in the Middle East—less than 1 percent. Although tourism took up only 1.4 percent of the overall share of transnational activity in developing countries, it was a significant share of such corporations' activities in the tourist economies of the Caribbean and South Pacific.[68] Although we do not have complete data on this, in some cases it was as high as 80 percent.[69]

COUNTRY BREAKDOWN OF
PRODUCTION ACTIVITIES

A country breakdown of activities of transnational corporations through foreign direct investment in developing countries is shown in Table 4.4. The following picture emerges (based mainly on data for 1967): Latin America and the Caribbean accounted for more than half of the value of transnational corporation activities in developing countries. This activity represented U.S. $18 billion out of the grand total of U.S. $33 billion. Next was Africa with roughly U.S. $6.6 billion, Asia with approximately U.S. $5 billion, and the Middle East with U.S. $3 billion. In terms of percentage share of parent countries of transnationals, the following was the picture to-

Table 4.4. Stock of Foreign Direct Investment in Developing Countries, by Country of Origin and Developing Region, End 1967

| | Region (percentage) | | | | |
Country[a]	Middle East	Asia[b]	Africa	Western Hemisphere[c]	Total
United States	57.3	35.6	20.8	63.8	50.4
United Kingdom	27.1	41.5	30.0	9.2	19.9
France	5.2	6.6	26.3	2.5	8.1
The Netherlands	5.6	5.1	4.9	5.1	5.1
Canada	0.2	1.0	0.7	7.3	4.4
Federal Republic of Germany	0.7	1.4	2.1	4.3	3.1
Japan	2.7	3.9	0.2	2.2	2.1
Italy	0.8	0.6	3.8	2.1	2.1
Belgium	0.1	0.3	7.3	0.6	1.9
Switzerland	0.2	1.4	0.9	2.3	1.7
Other[d]	0.1	2.6	3.0	0.6	1.3
Total (millions of dollars)	3,102.7	4,991.5	6,591.1	18,449.3	33,134.6

Source: Centre for Development Planning, Projections and Policies of the Department of Economic and Social Affairs of the UN Secretariat, based on OECD, Stock of Private Direct Investments by DAC Countries in Developing Countries, End 1967 (Paris, 1972).
[a]Countries are listed in descending order of total stock of foreign direct investment in developing countries.
[b]Including the developing countries of Oceania.
[c]Including the Caribbean region.
[d]Australia, Austria, Denmark, Norway, Portugal, and Sweden.

ward the end of 1960: The United States accounted for over 50 percent of total investment in developing countries; United Kingdom, 20 percent; France, 8 percent; the Netherlands, 5 percent; Canada, 4.4 percent; Federal Republic of Germany, 3.1 percent; Japan, 2.1 percent; Italy, 2.1 percent; Belgium, 1.9 percent; and Switzerland, 1.7 percent.[70] At the same time, the regional distribution was as follows: In the Middle East the greatest source of foreign direct investment through transnationals was the United States (57 percent), followed by the United Kingdom (27 percent), the Netherlands (6 percent), France (5 percent), and Japan (3 percent). In Asia the most important country was the United Kingdom (42 percent), then the United States (36 percent), France (7 percent), the Netherlands (5 percent), and Japan (4 percent). In Africa the United Kingdom was the largest supplier of foreign capital (30 percent), followed by France (26 percent), the United States (21 percent), Belgium (7 percent), the Netherlands (5 percent), and Italy (3.8 percent). In Latin America and the Caribbean, the United States ranked highest with 64 percent, followed by the United Kingdom (9.2 percent), Canada (7.3 percent), the Netherlands (5.1 percent), Germany (4.3 percent), France (2.5 percent), Switzerland (2.3 percent), and Japan (2.2 percent).

Table 4.5 shows that in 1971 roughly U.S. $4 billion was invested in developing countries, mainly through transnationals. Out of this, U.S. $2 billion was invested by the United States, U.S. $357 million by the United Kingdom, U.S. $283 million by the Netherlands, U.S. $248 million by Germany, and U.S. $236 million by Japan. Italy and France were next, with U.S. $194 million and U.S. $158 million, respectively. We are not in a position to compare trends from this, as the data pertain to just a single year. Nevertheless, it does give a broad idea of the relative importance of parent companies for that year.

On the whole, 1970–71 represented the highest growth year for foreign direct investment through transnationals, using 1960–61 as the base year. Between 1960 and 1961 the average annual growth of overseas investment in developing countries was 21.6 percent. Compare this with 23.5 percent during 1970–71. Between 1965 and 1966 the annual growth rate was 22.5 percent. Foreign direct investment involving transnationals tends to show a strong colonial association in many instances—hence, the relevance at times of historical and political considerations to its analysis. For example, U.K. investment in English-speaking Africa represented the following percentages of overall host-country shares accounted for by foreign capital: Nigeria, 57 percent; Ghana, 59 percent; Zambia, 80 percent; Kenya, 79 percent; Sierra Leone, 84 percent; Tanzania, 47 percent; Uganda, 48 percent; Sudan, 75 percent; Malawai, 93 percent; Swaziland, 97 percent; Botswana,

Table 4.5. Foreign Direct Investment Flows to Developing Countries: Rate of Growth and Ratio to Total Capital Flows, 1960–1971

Country[a]	Direct Investment, 1971 (millions of dollars)	Annual Rate of Change 1960–61 (average to 1970–71 average)	Direct Investment as Percentage of Total Flow		
			1960–61 (average)	1965–66 (average)	1970–71 (average)
United States	2,210.0	10.7	18.2	22.6	32.2
United Kingdom	357.0	3.3	31.4	22.9	25.7
The Netherlands	282.7	8.4	47.2	41.1	47.5
Federal Republic of Germany	247.8	14.3	10.5	16.6	19.4
Japan	235.5	11.0	36.5	19.0	12.7
Italy	193.7	9.8	31.3	11.7	21.0
France	157.5	−5.1	23.5	26.6	11.8
Canada	76.0	13.8	17.4	15.9	11.4
Switzerland	65.7	2.3	26.6	35.0	36.6
Sweden	40.1	1.8	70.2	27.8	18.1
Australia	40.0	48.0	1.7	10.8	15.9
Belgium	26.2	0.4	19.1	32.3	11.5
Norway	13.3	—	—	6.9	22.5
Denmark	10.0	12.6	10.2	−1.3	8.4
Portugal	2.0	—	—	25.6	3.1
Austria	−0.1	—	—	5.0	2.2
Total DAC countries	3,957.5	7.9	21.6	22.4	23.6
Total other[b]	8.0	4.1	11.3	292.7	7.0
Total developed market economy countries	3,965.5	7.9	21.6	22.5	23.5

Source: Centre for Development Planning, Projections and Policies of the Department of Economic and Social Affairs of the UN Secretariat, based on data from the Development Assistance Committee of OECD (Paris, 1972), with some adjustments and estimates.
[a] Countries are arranged in descending order of amount of direct investment in 1971.

88 percent; Gambia, 87 percent; and Lesotho, 60 percent. For France investment was the following in French-speaking Africa: Gabon, 73 percent; Ivory Coast, 80 pecent; Senegal, 87 percent; Cameroon, 75 percent; Mauritania, 69 percent; Congo, 83 percent; Malagasy, 76 percent; Togo, 57 percent; Central African Republic, 92 percent; Niger, 96 percent; Dahomey, 57 percent; Chad, 80 percent; Upper Volta, 75 percent; Mali, 77 percent; French Antilles, 72 percent; and French Guyana, 100 percent. In the case of Belgium, investment was similarly highest in its former colonies. For instance, Zaire had 88 percent, Rwanda had 87 percent, and Burundi had 85 percent.[71]

A main exception to the rule of historically determined foreign investment dominance involving transnationals was the United States. In the Middle East, the Caribbean, and Latin America, where it did not have colonies, U.S. foreign investment as a percentage of total foreign direct investment ranged between 70 and 90 percent.[72] However, it is misleading to interpret this information too generally, as cases exist apart from that of the United States in which investment by transnationals does not appear to be conditioned mainly by historical links. Colonial relationships may surely give a transnational of a metropolitan country some insight into the market of a country that was formerly colonized or remains colonized. But these are certainly not the only considerations that enter into the picture, even though they may give some transnationals strategic advantages over others in their attempts at a "global reach." For example, other considerations are access to certain raw materials, favorable political reception, favorable inducements to invest, familiarity with a given market, and some cultural insights, but the sword can indeed cut either way.[73]

A number of politically independent developing countries have shown an antagonistic attitude to transnationals originating from former metropolitan countries, as compared to those emanating from what may be considered to be politically more neutral countries—for instance, Japan, Germany, Switzerland, and Scandinavia.

TRANSNATIONAL CORPORATIONS AND IMPORTS

Typically, developing countries obtain well over 80 percent of their annual import requirements from developed countries. For the years 1970, 1972, and 1973, see Table 4.6 for some idea of this phenomenon. Table 4.7 provides a breakdown of commodity classes for the year 1973. Evidence from previous years suggests a similar pattern of imports in terms of the relative importance of respective commodity groups.[74] Table 4.7 shows that two

Table 4.6. Imports of Developing Countries' Manufactures and Semimanufactures, Selected Years

Year	Total (millions of dollars)	Developed Market Economy Countries (millions of dollars)	Share (percentage)
1970	44,200[a]	38,400	86
1972	52,764[b]	44,211	84
1973	71,176[b]	59,653	84

Source: UN, Monthly Bulletin of Statistics (December 1971); and provisional UNCTAD Secretariat estimates.
[a]SITC (Standard International Trade Classification) 5 to 8 plus 0 + 1.
[b]SITC 5 to 8 less 68.

commodity groups—machinery and transport equipment and other manufactured goods—dominate the import structure of developing countries as a group. These groups together accounted for some 70 percent of total imports of developing countries from developed ones. The United States, France, the United Kingdom, Germany, Japan, and the Netherlands together account for the bulk of developing countries' imports from developed countries.[75]

Let us examine the evidence of the role of transnationals in the manufactured imports of developing countries. This is the main form of imports of developing countries from developed ones. Technically, this examination would involve obtaining some statistical indication of activities of transnational corporations in developing countries' imports of manufactures and semimanufactures from developed market-economy countries. Unfortunately, such an exercise is severely limited because such data are usually not available from conventional trade statistics. Consequently, the evidence about to be presented is meant to be crudely illustrative. Attention is focused on two areas. The first area is the transnationality of exports of manufactures and semimanufactures from developed market-economy countries, and the second area is the corresponding product groups representing such transnationalized exports.

Recent evidence suggests that transnational corporations of the United States on average account for over 70 percent of total exports of manufactures and semimanufactures for that country.[76] In some product groups the export share of transnational corporations is above average. For example, in 1970 when U.S. transnational corporations exported U.S. $21.7 billion, or 58 percent of that country's exports of manufactured goods, the transna-

Table 4.7.   Selected Breakdown of Leading Manufactured and Semimanufactured Imports of Developing Countries from Developed Market Economy Countries, 1973

Developing Country	Commodity Classes (millions of dollars)				
	1	*2*	*3*	*4*	*5*
All developing countries	8,920	8,060	31,360	19,260	5,310
Africa	2,050	1,420	8,070	3,910	920
Latin America	2,550	2,940	9,800	5,230	1,550
Middle East	1,000	1,020	4,700	3,180	940
Asia	3,100	2,640	8,549	6,710	1,860

Source: UN, *Monthly Bulletin of Statistics* (various issues, 1974).
Key:
1 = food.
2 = chemicals.
3 = machineries and transport equipment.
4 = other manufactured goods.
5 = iron and steel products.

tionality of manufactured exports was as follows: primary and fabricated metals, 75 percent; electrical equipment and apparatus, 80 percent; industrial chemicals, 72 percent; office machines, 68 percent; electrical machinery, 66 percent; food products, 63 percent; and other manufacturing, 69 percent. At the same time, 274 transnational corporations were responsible for over 90 percent of the transnationally generated exports of manufactured products. As a group, they accounted for 50 percent of U.S. exports of manufactures.[77] This concentration ratio of transnationalized exports is in fact broadly correspondent to the concentration ratio of foreign direct investment by U.S. transnational corporations. For example, less than 300 U.S. transnational corporations account for over 70 percent of foreign direct investment for U.S. transnational corporations as a group.[78]

Considered in international terms (U.S.- plus overseas-based operations), global exports of U.S. transnational corporations amounted to nearly U.S. $38.7 billion, or about 20 percent of the world trade of manufactures and semimanufactures. The main export platform of U.S. transnational corporations is developed market-economy countries (OECD).[79] In 1970, U.S. transnationals based in the OECD countries exported U.S. $37.4 billion, or 97 percent of their world exports of manufactures. This is not surprising if consideration is given to the fact that foreign subsidiaries and affiliates of U.S. transnational corporations are located mainly in developed market-economy countries.

Looking at the export product breakdown of U.S. transnational corporations operating in OECD countries as a whole, the following picture emerges: While figures for 1970 show that these transnational corporations accounted for about 21 percent of OECD exports of manufactured products, the export share in some product groups runs far higher. For example, U.S. transnational corporations exported 42 percent of OECD transport equipment exports, 76 percent of its electrical equipment, 46 percent of its grain mill products, 39 percent of its soap and cosmetics, 34 percent of its farm machinery, 31 percent of its office machines, and 30 percent of its electrical equipment, as well as drugs.[80]

All in all, statistics on U.S. transnational corporations seem to indicate an active export involvement on the part of such transnational corporations in such product groups as food, chemicals and allied products, and machinery and transport equipment, which significantly enough represent the main import items of manufactures and semimanufactures by developing countries.

The foregoing pattern regarding the influence of U.S. transnational corporations on that country's exports of manufactures and semimanufactures or world imports of such products also seems to apply to the United Kingdom, the Federal Republic of Germany, and France, whose transnational corporations, together with those of the United States, account for over 90 percent of the book value of the existing world stock of foreign direct investments.[81]

Accordingly, about 80 percent of U.K. exports of manufactured goods are generated by transnational corporations—55 percent accountable to its own transnational corporations with the remaining 25 percent accountable to foreign transnational corporations. U.S. transnational corporations account for about 17 percent of such manufactured exports from the United Kingdom. Simultaneously, about 200 U.K. transnational corporations account for about 50 percent of that country's manufactured exports, and about 12 of these corporations account for as much as 20 percent.[82] The export influence of these transnational corporations, like that of their counterparts in the United States, is felt particularly in the areas of food, chemicals, machinery and transport equipment, and other manufactured goods. It is also of interest to note that 175 U.K. transnational corporations control over 80 percent of total overseas investments, with 30 of these corporations accounting for nearly 50 percent of that country's manufacturing activities in developing countries.[83]

Likewise, in the Federal Republic of Germany, 100 transnational corporations exported over 50 percent of that country's manufactured exports in the 1960s. By 1971, 27 of these corporations accounted for nearly 35 percent of that country's manufactured exports. These 27 corporations' export share of selected products was as follows: chemicals, 65 percent; electrical products, 56 percent; and motor vehicles, 64 percent.[84] At the same time, they accounted for 60–70 percent of total West German direct investment in foreign manufacturing production.[85]

Comparable data are not available for France, but a similar situation seems to prevail there, both in terms of the influence of transnational corporations on France's exports of manufactures (especially in the area of chemicals, machinery and transport equipment, and electrical equipment) and in terms of the concentration ratio of foreign direct investment by transnational corporations of that country. The same is also true of other European countries, such as Sweden; 75 percent of that country's exports are generated by transnational corporations. The export performance of Switzerland and the Netherlands, according to recent data, seems to indicate a similar tendency of transnational dominance.[86]

In the case of Japan, the major transnational trading companies accounted for over 50 percent of export trade in 1972. Metals, machinery, textiles, and food are the main product areas of these trading companies. Recent evidence also points to the presence of transnational marketing corporations in other developed countries.[87]

Since the developed market-economy countries cited here supply the bulk of developing countries' overall import demand of manufactured and semimanufactured goods, a reasonable argument seems to be that the transnational corporations of these countries play an important role in developing countries' imports of such products.

Additionally, developed countries trade with each other. In 1970, for instance, developing countries imported over U.S. $6 billion in manufactures and semimanufactures from other developing countries. Such imports were made up largely of electrical equipment, motor vehicles and other transport equipment, textiles, and other light manufacturing products that represent productive activity on the part of transnational corporations operating in these countries. Naturally, account must be taken of this in terms of the overall role of transnational corporations in the imports of manufactures and semimanufactures of developing countries. Unfortunately, no precise estimates are available as to the impact of transnational corporations in interdeveloping country trade, though one suspects that it is by no means insignificant.

Evidence also points to the fact that such imports involving transnationals often involve intrafirm transfers rather than arms-length trade. In some sectors—notably, transport equipment, electrical machinery, and chemicals—import demand in the form of intrafirm sales can be as high as 90 percent of the total sectoral requirements that are imported.[88] There is, however, a danger in generalizing this situation in terms of the extent of intracorporate trade, especially since data are at times neither fully reliable nor available.

TRANSNATIONAL CORPORATIONS AND EXPORTS

Developing countries' exports that involve transnational corporations fall into four broad categories as follows:

Exports of raw materials, such as agricultural ones (coffee, tea, sugar, rice, and so on) and minerals (copper, tin, bauxite, petroleum, zinc, and so on) in crude or processed form;
Conversion of import substitution to exports;
Exports of labor-intensive final products embodying unskilled labor;
Specialized labor-intensive manufacturing activities of processes geared for export within the context of vertically integrated transnational firms, to which some reference was made earlier.

Reference was made to the last three categories in the previous discussion of production activities of transnationals in developing countries.

Data are available for countries that together accounted for 80 percent of developing countries' exports of manufactured goods in the late 1960s.[89] These data pertain mainly to the last export category—specialized labor-intensive activities. In such countries as Hong Kong, Taiwan, South Korea, Mexico, and India, manufactured exports of transnationals, as a percentage of total exports, ranged between 67 percent and 27 percent, as Table 4.8 shows. The table further shows that between 1962 and 1969, the export growth rate of manufactured goods was as high as 77 percent in one case and over 10 percent in most cases. Most of the exports went to the United States. Intrafirm transfers were reported to be highly significant.[90] A main factor accounting for this are provisions 806.30 and 807.00 of the U.S. Tariff Schedules. These provisions permit import duties to be leveled only upon one value created abroad when inputs have been supplied by the United States.[91] Imports from developing countries cited in Table 4.8 rose under the tariff schedules from U.S. $61 million to U.S. $539 million between

Table 4.8. Manufactured Exports and Total Exports from Selected Less-Developed Countries

Country	Value of Manufactured Exports (millions of dollars) 1969	Manufacturing, as Percentage of Total Exports 1969	Increases in Manufacturing as Percentage of Increases in Total Exports 1962-1969	Manufacturing Export Growth Rate (percentage) 1962-1969	Total Export Growth Rate (percentage) 1960-1970	1965-1970
Hong Kong	1,484	67.4	76.0	20.1	13.8	17.1
Taiwan	570	57.0	60.8	36.5	24.2	26.0
India	547	30.0	42.4	6.1	3.9	3.0
Yugoslavia	513	34.2	42.1	15.9	11.5	9.0
Mexico	380	27.0	52.5	19.8	6.2	4.5
South Korea	365	60.8	63.2	77.1	38.2	36.7
Brazil	244	10.6	14.4	16.2	8.0	11.4
Argentina	208	13.0	28.2	11.7	5.0	3.4
Pakistan	197	28.1	53.3	23.7	6.3	6.5
Philippines	138	15.3	16.6	10.2	6.6	6.8
Iran	133	6.3	5.1	8.7	10.9	12.7
Malaysia	130	8.1	n.a.	18.0	3.6	6.5
Nigeria	38	4.2	6.0	18.1	10.1	10.6
United Arab Republic	33	4.7	6.1	4.8	3.0	4.7
Colombia	26	4.3	13.1	19.6	4.8	16.8
Chile	23	2.0	1.8	8.4	9.2	11.4
Indonesia	20	2.8	9.5	21.3	3.9	7.6

Source: G. K. Helleiner, "Manufactured Exports from Less Developed Countries and Multinational Firms," Economic Journal (March 1973): 24.

Note: Manufactured exports exclude petroleum products and unworked nonferrous metals. Country selection is based upon ready availability of comparable data.

1960 and 1970, or from 4 percent to over 14 percent of overall exports of manufactured goods from less-developed countries to developed economies.[92]

So far, for one range of exports, UNCTAD has provided some evidence on the role of transnationals in the total exports of manufactured goods of developing countries as a group. The evidence, which is based on figures for 1975, indicates that such corporations accounted for some 50 percent of all exports of manufactured goods from developing countries.[93] Even so, it is dangerous to offer broad generalizations. We present the following statistical findings on the role of transnationals in the exports of manufactured goods of some developing countries for earlier periods to illustrate this point:

In Argentina it was found that in 1969 transnational corporations accounted for about 30 percent of that country's manufactured exports.[94]

Fajnzbler concluded in a recent study that in 1969 transnational corporations accounted for nearly 44 percent of Brazil's exports of manufactured goods.[95] U.S. transnational corporations accounted for the bulk of transnationalized exports. In 1970 they accounted for nearly 26 percent or U.S. $145 million of Brazil's total exports of manufactured goods of U.S. $564 million.

A study on quantifiable trade features of Colombia estimates that transnational corporations sold 35 percent of total manufactured exports of Colombia in 1970.[96] Another sample-based study conducted ten years earlier found the percentage share of transnational corporations in Colombia's manufactured exports to be in the vicinity of 20 percent.[97]

For Hong Kong, two hundred transnational corporations in 1970 accounted for 12 percent or U.S. $239 million of total manufactured exports worth U.S. $2.1 billion.[98] When consideration is given to the sum total of operating transnational corporations and the role of transnational marketing corporations, this figure is likely to be somewhat of an underestimate.

In India data for the 1960s reveal that transnational corporations accounted for less than 10 percent of that country's exports of manufactured goods. Between 1966 and 1967 it was 7.2 percent, and during the period 1960–1961 to 1966–1967 the average export share was 6.9 percent.[99]

Data available for Mexico indicate that in 1970 manufacture affiliates of U.S. transnational corporations accounted for 30 percent of that country's manufactured exports.[100] A major part of these exports are under offshore assembly provisions. In 1971, for example, such exports were 26 percent or U.S. $175 million of total manufactured exports worth U.S. $667 million.[101]

In the case of Pakistan, available provisional data suggest that the role of transnational corporations in the exports of manufactures and semimanufactures is less than 10 percent.

Data compiled by the Board of Investments in the Philippines indicate that transnational corporations account for 20-25 percent of that country's exports of manufactured goods.[102]

Statistical evidence on Singapore reveals that transnational corporations account for at least 50 percent of that country's manufactured exports, made up largely of processing and assembling activities.[103]

In 1970, transnational corporations accounted for 15 percent of total exports of manufactured goods of South Korea.[104]

In the case of Taiwan's exports, available data suggest that 12-15 percent of manufactured exports are attributable to transnational corporations.[105]

Intrafirm transactions account for a sizable proportion of the exports of subsidiaries and affiliates of U.S. transnational corporations. Earlier we noted the importance of intrafirm transactions in developing countries' imports. In 1970 majority-owned affiliates of 298 U.S. transnational corporations exported U.S. $12.6 billion, of which intracompany transactions to the parent company and other affiliates were U.S. $7.1 billion, or 57 percent of total exports.[106] At the same time, the percentage of intragroup exports to overall exports of subsidiaries and affiliates of U.S. transnational corporations in developing countries was nearly 90 percent for transport equipment, over 84 percent for electrical equipment and electronic parts, 72 percent for textiles and apparel, and 64 percent for instruments.

Data available on transnational corporations of the Federal Republic of Germany operating in developing countries indicate that intragroup exports as a percentage of total manufactured exports of subsidiaries or affiliates of five developing countries were nearly 60 percent in 1971.[107] In Mexico this percentage was as high as 80 percent, and in Argentina it was 62 percent. In India the percentage share was below average at 29 percent.[108] As far as the operations of U.K. transnational corporations in developing countries are concerned, intragroup manufactured exports as a percentage of total transnational exports was estimated at 14 percent. In the case of food, drink, and tobacco, however, it was 69 percent.[109]

The estimates of the role of transnational corporations in the exports of manufactures and semimanufactures presented in this section do not generally include the role of transnational marketing corporations, which are regarded by several trade commentators as an important vehicle in the export expansion of such products from developing countries. In Asia, for example, Japanese transnational marketing corporations are regarded as "the real key to expansion in manufactured goods."[110] Transnational marketing corporations are also active in the exports of manufactures and semimanufactures of developing countries in Latin America and Africa. However, data are not available as to their real impact in terms of overall manufactured exports of developing countries.

In some product groups, especially in primary agriculture and mining, transnationals were reported to exert important influences on exports. For example, in the case of food preparations and copper, transnationals were reported to control over 90 percent of what developing countries sell to the world economy. The same held for copper. In the case of aluminum, iron, and worked ores, transnationals were estimated to control about 90 percent. In the case of tobacco, tea, tin, and coffee, export control by transnationals was estimated at 70 percent, 60 percent, and 55 percent, respectively.[111]

5 RESTRICTIVE BUSINESS PRACTICES AND TRANSNATIONAL CORPORATIONS:
Some Available Evidence

An important point of departure in the study of restrictive business practices, as was demonstrated earlier, is the concept of market power. The link between market power and the study of transnationals has already been shown. A firm may use a number of restrictive business practices as a means of consolidating market power—for example, collusive pricing arrangements, entry-forestalling techniques, freezing marketing and distribution channels, tying firms to sources of supplies, and the like. This chapter looks at the various practices by transnationals for extending market power in developing countries.

TYPES OF RESTRICTIVE BUSINESS PRACTICES

In Chapter 1 we looked at some of the restrictive business practices that are found in textbook analyses of firm behavior. In terms of the operations of transnational corporations in developing countries, however, the available empirical evidence suggests that restrictive business practices take on a more complex and wide-ranging character.

Usually restrictive business practices may be regarded as vertical, horizontal, or conglomerate. This would follow from the prevailing literature on industrial organization. Vertical practices would involve enterprises engaged in different phases of a production process—for example, plantation-oriented transnationals. Horizontal practices would be relevant where practices affect similar product groups. Merger activity affecting such firms would fall into this category if it is intended to restrict competition. The conglomerate type of restrictive business practices would involve firms in distinct product lines. Those affecting multiproduct firms would seem relevant here.

Broadly speaking, the evidence suggests that restrictive business practices of transnational corporations in developing countries can be classified into the following areas: aspects of pricing policies, territorial market and product allocation arrangements, and forms of boycotts or enforcement measures.[1] The literature suggests that pricing policies and territorial market and product allocation arrangements are often important elements of the corporate strategies of transnational corporations.[2] These elements are closely related to the long-run strategies of maximizing profits, market growth, and stability, among other things, globally. Boycotts and other measures are practices that may be adopted by dominant firms, either singly or collusively, to ensure that agreements are complied with, as well as to keep competitors out of particular markets. Also, strategies involving their use may be defensive or predatory.[3] In the former case, the attempt is largely to protect markets or sources of raw materials; in the latter case, the attempt is largely to get rid of competition and to dominate a particular market.

A recent UN study has identified strategies relating to prices and territorial and product allocation arrangements as constituting the core of restrictive business practices of transnational corporations.[4] The following categories of practices have been identified:

Practices relating to imports and exports;
Practices on the levels of production and types of productive activities;
Practices on the purchase of capital equipment and inputs used in productive activity by subsidiaries and affiliates of transnationals;
Practices relating to the use of industrial property rights as well as know-how;
Practices in which firms outside the corporation will act as distributors for their products including (1) regulations concerning the purchase of products other than those that are the principal object of the arrangement, (2) restrictions on handling or manufacturing competing prod-

ucts, (3) restrictions on the types of customers to use imported products, and (4) refusals to sell or supply products to other firms.[5]

In connection with territorial and product allocation arrangements, the study notes the following practices as they affect mergers and acquisitions:

Practices carried out by corporations in connection with the expansion and diversification of activities nationally and internationally;
Practices carried out by firms that affect competitors and partners in particular markets.[6]

The following two broad groups of pricing policies have been also identified:

Transfer prices to be charged for intracorporate transactions;
Fixing of prices to be charged to arms-length purchases, including the fixing of sale and resale prices for products imported and exported.[7]

An expert group on restrictive business practices has added finer content to the restrictive business practices of transnational corporations in developing countries.[8] The practices are grouped into national external-trade cartels, international cartels, domestic restrictive business practices, and acquisition or abuse of a dominant position or acts of unfair competition. In terms of international and national external-trade cartels, the following specific practices have been identified:

Agreements fixing price as to exports and imports;
Collusive tendering;
Market or customer allocation arrangements;
Allocation by quota as to sales and production;
Collective action to enforce arrangements.

The following practices have been identified in the case of domestic practices:

Price fixing and rebate cartels, collusive tendering, resale price maintenance, and other collusive arrangements;
Collective boycotts;
Denial of access to an association, joint arrangement, or facility that is crucial to competition.

The main practices identified in terms of acquisition or abuse of dominant positions are

Anticompetitive exclusive dealing and anticompetitive refusals to deal;
Unnecessarily tied sales or purchases;
Predatory or discriminatory pricing;
Anticompetitive mergers, takeovers, or other acquisitions.

Fine has also identified a number of practices in international trade that point to pricing, product, and market allocation arrangements as the overriding considerations.[9] They are

Practices aimed at influencing prices or conditions of sale, purchase, or release, such as speculative schemes, concerted price fixing, or non-concerted price fixing;
The limitation or production and restriction of productive capacity or of the number of varieties produced;
Market allocation that can be either territorial allocation or allocation of different lines of production;
Establishment of joint purchasing or sales or profit-pooling arrangements;
Restrictions on matters of technological research, patents, and the like;
Practices aimed at eliminating external competition;
Combinations of all elements listed.

A large number of restrictive business practices have also been identified in relation to the acquisition of technology by developing countries through transnational corporations. Such practices include

Restrictions on the recipient's volume, scope, range of production, or field of activity;
Restrictions on obtaining competing or complementary technology through patents and know-how from other sources;
Limitations by the supplier regarding the sources of supply of raw materials, spare parts, intermediate products, and capital goods;
Use of quality controls or standards by the technology supplier as a means of imposing unnecessary obligations on the technology recipients;
Limitations upon the diffusion and/or further use of technology already imported, thus requiring additional payments for repeated use of the same technology;

Requirements that the recipient pay royalties during the entire duration of manufacture of a product or the application of the process involved and, therefore, without any specification of time;

Prohibitions or restrictions on the use of the technology after the normal expiration of the arrangement;

Use of the privilege granted under the trademark system to restrict unduly the recipient's activities;

Prohibitions or limitations of any type on the export of products manufactured on the basis of the technology supplied, including restrictions on exports to certain markets, permission to export only to certain markets, and requirements of prior approval of the supplier for exports and prices of exported products;

Restrictions on the freedom of the recipient to enter into sales or representation agreements related to similar technologies or products;

Requirements that the recipient of technology give exclusive sales or representation rights to the supplier, with due regard to subcontracting arrangements;

Reservation of the right by the supplier to fix the sale or resale of the products manufactured;

Requirements prohibiting or restricting exports by the recipient of goods covered by a trademark arrangement;

Tying of the supply of imports of a product bearing a particular trademark to the trademark owner and thereby the prohibiting of imports from a third party or another licensee;

Regulations that restrict or subject to approval by the supplier the publicity or advertisement to be carried out by the recipient;

Obligation of the recipient to convert technology payments into capital stock;

Continuation of payments for unused or unexploited technology;

Requirements that additional technology not desired by the recipient or needed in the recipient country, such as consultancy services, international subcontracting, turnkey projects, and various forms of package arrangements, be accepted as a condition for obtaining the technology;

Tying of the imports of inputs, equipment, and spare parts, as well as technical and managerial personnel, to a specific external source, thus making it possible for enterprises to charge higher than normal prices for them;

Requirements of payments by the recipient enterprises for technology imported by the enterprise under earlier arrangements or already available in the country;

Increased rates of payment imposed by the technology supplier upon the technology recipient for output of earmarked export, vis à vis domestic sales, except in cases in which such differential rates are in the interest of the recipient country;

Charging fixed minimum payments irrespective of production performance and/or increasing royalty rates progressively with the rise in the scale of output;

Charging royalties or fees for know-how of technical assistance in a cumulative way on parts as well as on the final product so that the total charges are in fact larger than if the same percentage were applied on a net value–added basis;

Limitations on the research and development policy and activities of the recipient enterprise;

Grant-back provisions establishing a unilateral flow of technical information and improvements from the technology recipient without reciprocal obligations from the technology supplier;

Requirements to use personnel designated by the technology suppliers beyond the period sufficient for the training of the recipient's personnel, or limitations in the use of personnel of the recipient country;

Requirements by the supplier, except in management contracts, to participate in the management decisions of the recipient enterprise;

Obligations upon the recipient to purchase further inventions and improvements in the technology from the original supplier;

Limitation upon the access of the recipient to new technological developments and improvements related to the technology supplied;

Restriction upon the recipient from adapting the imported technology to local conditions and innovating on the supplied technology;

Obligation upon the recipient to introduce unnecessary design changes and new material specifications imposed by the technology supplier;

Agreement by the recipient not to contest the validity of the patents involved;

Unduly long duration of contractual agreements or arrangements;

Restriction of the field of use of the subject matter of a patent and of any unpatented know-how license related to the working of the patent;

Charging of royalties on patents and other industrial property rights after their expiration, termination, or invalidation;

Exemption of the supplier from any liability consequent upon defects in the goods produced by the recipient with the help of the technology acquired;

Charging of royalties on patents and other industrial property rights not registered in the recipient's countries;

Other limitations having adverse effects on the recipient and imposed as a condition for obtaining the technology acquired.[10]

Indications from the available data seem to indicate that vertical considerations play an important part in the restrictive business practices of transnationals that are relevant to development problems. This would seem to follow from the existence of a large number of vertically integrated transnationals as they affect economic activity in such countries. However, more research is needed to establish this point rigorously.

RESTRICTIVE BUSINESS PRACTICES AND TRANSNATIONAL CORPORATIONS: THE FACTUAL SITUATION

This section attempts to look at some of the effects of market dominance by modern corporations as they relate to the restrictive business practices of transnational firms in developing countries. We have already established the importance of restrictive practices in the competitive process of market-dominating firms.

Most studies on restrictive business practices of transnationals in developing countries tend to ignore the primary sector. This lack, for example, is evident in UNCTAD's work. Here most of the attention on restrictive business practices has focused on the manufacturing sector. However, this approach may be considered too narrow. As we will show presently, such practices have been widespread in traditional forms of the activity of transnational corporations, such as plantations and mining.

Traditional Activity of Transnational Corporations

Mining and plantations often involve subsidiaries of transnationals rather than forms of collaboration with local enterprises, such as joint ventures. This situation has been changing slightly of late since several governments have moved to take an active part in the natural resource sector. Almost invariably, the interest of transnationals has been to export raw materials for further processing and refining abroad where market outlets for final products were largely found. Evidence suggests that uneven market forces have tended to be greater in this sector than in new activities of transnational corporations. Typically, as Vernon argues, "a small group of very large firms," has tended to characterize transnationals engaged in the raw material sector.[11] These include plantation agriculture, oil, copper, and aluminum, among others.

A large number of developing countries in Africa, the Caribbean, and parts of Asia have come to be called *plantation economies* because of the importance of the role that transnationals have played in the economic history of such countries.[12] Such enterprises include Booker McConnell, Tate and Lyle, Unilever, United Fruit, and United Brands. Often, plantations operated as vertically integrated enterprises. Their activities included shipping, manufacturing, engineering, marketing, and other services. A particular characteristic of plantation enterprises was the monopolization of large tracts of agricultural land and control over strategic inputs, such as irrigation, processing facilities, and access to credit.[13] Control over these facilities was often used to keep out competition, especially from peasant agriculture.[14]

The case of Jamaica documented by Beckford is probably indicative of the general pattern. He argues, "From the very outset peasant production in the West Indies had to compete with previously established plantations production for the very scarce resources, in particular labour and land. . . . The stranglehold of the plantations has remained to this very day and has served to limit the accessibility of resources to the peasants."[15] Beckford notes that the Jamaican peasantry has failed to achieve any meaningful portion of the country's agricultural land and other resources and that "what little they have achieved can hardly be maintained in the face of continuing stiff competition from the plantations."[16]

Two main factors, identified by Beckford, were responsible for the monopolization tendency found among transnationals engaged in plantation activities. They are

The need for increasing and maintaining market shares in increasingly differentiated product marketing;

Cumulative economies that began to arise once the enterprises began plantation production—for example, external economies, interindustry economies, skill economies, economies of diversification, economies of scale, fixed-capital economies, and market-infrastructure economies.[17]

Apart from attempts to stifle competition from peasants as such, an important consideration in plantation production, which has been documented in the literature, was the availability of ready sources of labor. To this end, the institution of slavery, for example, was strongly identified with plantation production in the New World.[18] With the emancipation of slaves, shortage of labor became a special problem. However, payment of higher wages not only served to induce labor from the peasant sector to the plantations but also to "destroy peasant production."[19] If peasant production continued unchecked, sources of labor supply for plantation agriculture would clearly have proven to be difficult. Hence, it could be argued, the need exists to control land and to bid labor away from the peasant sector.

Apart from labor-market considerations, other related considerations were equally relevant. In the case of Tate and Lyle, collusive mergers in the parent market—the United Kingdom—resulted in the amalgamation of two family refining companies "to cease competing and fight the foreigners by forming the biggest sugar company of the day. . . ."[20] In some cases, such as that of Booker McConnell, amalgamation of several foreign-owned small estates took place in various parts of the Caribbean.[21] This helped to reduce competition between rural plantation enterprises and in setting up plantation monopolies in several countries, such as Guyana. Further, changes in technology—namely, highly capital-intensive processes involving considerable economies of scale—meant that "the larger metropolitan concerns were able to eliminate weaker competitors in plantation production and to secure linkages associated with that production. . . ."[22]

Another writer, Kabunda, documents a similar monopolization process in the case of Unilever in Africa, which operated to the detriment of indigenous competitors. Unilever's history is strongly connected with soap. The background is as follows: In 1906 the soap sector underwent several crises that were to have particular consequences to the future of the firm and on its relations with Africa. The crises were partly due to the stabilization of the demand for soap on the British market, which was associated with sharp increases in the price of raw materials used in the manufacturer of soap. The firm was therefore no longer able to make high profits. The problem was compounded by increased competition from margarine manufacturers, on the one hand, and the very weak growth in supplies of raw materials, on the other.[23]

"These two phenomena," argued Kabunda, "seriously threatened the expansionist designs of William Lever who, confronted with this threat, set up trusts in Great Britain, purchasing the business of his competitors rather than battling with them to obtain large portions of the market."[24] Internationally, Lever attempted to contain the market crisis by increasing foreign investments in the manufacture and sale of soap in industrialized countries.

In Africa the enterprise sought to acquire its own sources of raw materials to enjoy the economy that vertical integration provided and to increase the world stock of its raw materials.[25] Acquisitions were particularly marked in Zaire, among other countries. As Kabunda notes, "As part of Unilever's strategy to obtain direct access to the raw materials and to maintain the monopoly of tropical seeds, the plantations of the Congo were the determining factors for supplying these raw materials at a very low price."[26] Raw materials included palm grove, rubber, cocoa, coffee, and tea. Accompanying this was a special process of monopolization of land and other resources. As Kabunda documents, "Unilever established plantations in complete ownership with the monopoly for the purchase of agricultural products from peasants at a low price, the monopoly for the treatment of these products, and monopoly for recruiting manpower."[27]

Kabunda has failed to offer an analysis of the specific forms of restrictive business practices used by Unilever first to penetrate the African economy and second to maintain market power there. Political factors were certainly important in the first instance—namely, the acquisition of agricultural land. The introduction of wage labor was also important, as in the case of the Caribbean, to attract labor away from other agricultural pursuits and to consolidate market power in African agriculture by limiting peasant production.

The banana industry in developing countries provides another example of the widespread use of restrictive business practices by transnational corporations. A recent study has shown the high concentration in the import markets for bananas from developing countries. Table 5.1 shows the role of transnationals in these markets.

Developing countries export the bulk of their annual banana production abroad. The main banana-producing countries are the Windward Islands, Jamaica, Panama, Costa Rica, Ecuador, Honduras, Somalia, Colombia, the Ivory Coast, and the Philippines. Transnationals have dominated in the production of bananas in each of these countries. Estimates for 1970 show the percentage of aggregate exports controlled by transnationals in these countries: Windward Islands, 48 percent; Panama, 59 percent; Costa Rica, 29 percent; Ecuador, 41 percent; Somalia, 31 percent. In terms of employment, the share of transnationals in the agricultural labor force in these countries was Windward Islands, 60 percent; Jamaica, 54 percent; Panama, 49 percent; Costa Rica, 45 percent; Ecuador, 31 percent; and Honduras, 22 percent.[28]

A number of restrictive business practices associated with import cartels involving transnationals were mentioned earlier. We do not have actual evidence to support the incidence of restrictive business practices by transnationals engaged in the banana trade. This, however, should not be ruled out, as evidence suggests their use in domestic markets in developing countries. A case in point is the United Fruit Company (UFC) in Latin America.

Table 5.1.   Transnationals and the Banana Import Trade, 1970–1972

Country	Percentage
Canada	100
United States	90
Switzerland	89
Belgium	78
Italy	78
The Netherlands	72
Germany	70
United Kingdom	40

Source: UNCTAD, *Marketing and Distribution System for Bananas* (Geneva, 1974).

A legal action was filed against that company for the widespread use of restrictive business practices. The complaint against the United Fruit Company read, "With the exception of land in Ecuador, UFC owns, leases, or
otherwise controls 85 percent of the land in the American tropics suitable
for banana cultivation."[29] The complaint argued that UFC had contracted,
combined, and conspired to restrain interstate and foreign trade in bananas
and had monopolized such trade over a number of years.[30] It was further
alleged that "by numerous clauses relating to coercing, agreeing, combining, or contracting, in a manner considered to constitute unreasonable restraints to trade, concealing ownership of proprietary interest, acquiring
ownership of competing banana enterprises, and engaging in various specified trade practices, the company was able to consolidate its market power
worldwide."[31] Trends in concentration in land ownership in Central
America, the Caribbean, as well as parts of Africa, which possibly involved
the use of a number of restrictive business practices, were also identified.[32]
    In the case of cocoa, a recent study shows that in terms of sales of de-
veloping countries abroad, a few oligopolies control the marketing and distribution networks. In the United States four companies are found to be responsible for the bulk of import trade through dealers and specialized
firms. In the United Kingdom four firms control nearly 80 percent of the
import market; in the Netherlands five firms control over 50 percent; in
France five firms control 51 percent; and in Belgium one firm controls 45
percent.[33] Competitive attrition, mergers, and outright purchases have
been identified as the main restrictive strategies adopted by transnational
corporations in the ongoing process of oligopolization. Such concentrated
buyers' power likely will reflect itself in prices that developing countries obtain for their cocoa exports. Such power clearly will introduce a form of

asymmetry in demand and supply relations. Little analysis has so far been conducted on identifying the role of buyer concentration in the overall price trends for cocoa and other primary exports of developing countries facing similar buyer-dominated markets.

Let us look at some available evidence pertaining to the mining sector. Penrose has noted that "cartel agreements, marketing alliances, price maintenance agreements, mergers and combinations" were among the restrictive business practices associated with the rise of major oil companies in developing countries.[34] She argues that "private monopolistic agreements may enable the foreign subsidiary to obtain a dominating position in an important industry or even in the economy as a whole. Such a situation is common in developing countries."[35] We are not aware of any systematic attempt at analyzing the use of restrictive business practices as a strategy for market control in oil-producing economies. It is probable that political considerations relating to the procurement of licensing agreements during the exploration phases and control over exploration and refining technologies during the production phases were among the factors that have helped oil companies to consolidate their market power in many developing countries, such as those in the Middle East, parts of Latin America, and a few in Africa, such as Gabon and Nigeria. Tanzer, meanwhile, has argued that the chief mechanism that has served to buttress the companies' monopoly control over the world's low-cost crude oil has been their high degree of vertical integration. Thus, "by the ownership of affiliated refining and marketing companies in various oil-importing countries, each company has secured captive outlets for the profitable crude which cannot be won away from them by competitors."[36]

Vernon has produced further evidence as to the occurrence of restrictive business practices in the rise of oil companies.[37] Between 1928 and 1948, cooperative measures involved the formation of international oil cartels, and after 1948, cooperation, in Vernon's words, "took forms which were much more complex in character."[38] A common method of pricing was set up that reduced the probability of any of the leaders offering crude oil or petroleum products that were greatly out of line with those agreed upon. Also, agreements included the purchase of surplus oil from "agreeing firms" and the swapping of supplies in different parts of the world.[39]

A similar experience is documented for copper and bauxite and characterized by oligopolies bent on "developing and controlling large, rich bodies of ore."[40] In the case of copper, formal cartels were set up between World War I and World War II by leading transnationals operating in developing countries. The idea was to fix prices, allocate production territorially and limit access to new firms. It is true, however, that copper had to reckon with competition from scrap copper and aluminum, which meant that the basis for monopolization was not as secure as with oil, for example. However, the oligopolistic market structure of the industry in worldwide terms was enough to foster agreements among dominant firms. Moreover, to hedge against risks, Vernon argues that a number of these companies began to diversify into other metals, including "the outstanding rival to copper—aluminum."[41]

In the case of bauxite, giant transnationals made their appearance in developing countries in the early twentieth century. For a number of years, U.S. corporations, such as ALCOA, ALCAN, Reynolds, Kaiser, and Chemical Corporation, were said to have operated a near monopoly over world production. They were later joined by European transnationals, such as Alusuisee and Pechiney. However, this move did little to alter the international structure of the industry. Together these transnationals own or control "most of the known bauxite deposits in developing countries."[42]

Efficient production of aluminum requires highly complex technology relating to smelters. The refining costs are quite high—namely, 60 percent of production costs, compared to 6–7 percent in the case of oil and 15 percent in the case of copper.[43] Also, a large quantity of electricity is normally required. This technological consideration no doubt served in part as a barrier to the entry of new firms. Collusive practices were, however, widespread. For example, cartel agreements were common before 1945. Later, the main participants of the industry formed partnerships, including those to operate joint bauxite mines and the operation of smelters. Vernon notes in this connection that until "the late 1960s there was scarcely a major aluminum producer in the world that did not have some fairly direct link with all the others."[44]

The tin industry provides another interesting example of the use of restrictive business practices by transnationals in order to establish themselves in developing countries. A case in point is Malaysia, where transnationals systematically displaced Chinese and Malays from ownership of vital deposits in Peruk and Selangor. Transnationals, largely European in origin, began operating in Malaysia in the late nineteenth century. By 1900 they were producing 10 percent of the total tin output in the country, and by 1963 a few transnationals were producing 75 percent of all output by foreign mines and 45 percent of total Malaysian output.[45] Interlocking directorates, forms of acquisition involving local tin producers, helped to foster a situation of "concentration of ownership and control of production."[46] However, Yip Hoong suggests that official policies have tended to favor transnationals in penetrating the local tin market. He records, "In granting licences to mines, the amount of capital which a mining firm could raise was one of the most important factors which influenced official decisions. Thus, as soon as this standard was applied, the foreign companies with their heavy investments in fixed capital had an advantage over small Chinese miners."[47] The argument further goes, "The early foreign mining companies were favorably assisted in their competition with the old, established Chinese tin miners by official policies aimed at encouraging the expansion of foreign tin mining in Malaysia at the expense of the Chinese."[48] This account merely points to the fact that public policy considerations sometimes played a role in promoting restrictive business strategies by transnationals. This support no doubt increased the competitive cutting edge of some transnationals.

We are not sure of the extent of the pricing policies of transnationals in reducing local competition. This occurrence, however, is not unlikely given the fact that smelting and refining soon came under the complete control of transnationals. Also, it is likely that wage payments might have played some role in the battle of the strong against the weak.

A number of cartel practices, in addition to those involving oil, bauxite, and copper, have been documented in the meantime. A well-known case involving developing countries was the coconut cartel. Five U.S. transnationals, including General Foods, which distributed 75 percent of coconut imported to the United States, were accused of price fixing and of attempting to monopolize trade.[49] The firms were charged with employing the following practices aimed at suppressing and eliminating competition:

Applying established freight and storage charges to the identical base prices and price schedules in order to achieve uniform prices and delivery terms;

Exchanging information concerning past, present, and future price policies;

Maintaining a price-leadership plan whereby the price leader announced price changes and other selling factors;

Eliminating competition by restricting sources of supply of competing processes and effectuating price squeezes.

In the consent judgment, the defendants were forbidden from engaging in these practices, as well as others deemed to restrict competition. A similar case was reported in connection with the export of molasses from the Caribbean.[50] The charge involved the largest transnational purchaser of domestic and offshore molasses in the United States—Southern Western Sugar and Molasses Company. The charges included the use of price discrimination and other acts aimed at eliminating and suppressing competition. The acts included

Persuasion, coercion, and compulsion by independent competitors to maintain and not to sell below prices established by the leading company;

Refusal to sell to violators of established prices.

Also, transnational firms were active members of the Bark Pool agreement, which was concerned with the fixing of prices for bark, the basic raw material used in the quinine industry, and which involved territorial market arrangements.[51] These included firms in the Congo and other parts of Africa, Indonesia, India, and South America. Certain transnational firms operating in developing countries, such as in parts of Africa, were prohibited from exporting quinine and quinidine. Further, part of the agreement was that all signatories except the French firms agreed not to sell to French African territories. A penalty was imposed on transnationals that oversupplied.[52]

Other cartels affecting raw materials from developing countries that have been in existence from time to time include phosphorous, potash, cement, coke, wood pulp, rubber, and the like. Basically the purpose of these cartels was to restrict production, to divide export markets, and to fix prices.[53] However, not all cartel-like arrangements, especially those of an informal nature, are recorded. This implies that such cartels may be more widespread than they seem to be at first sight. Further research is needed to establish the extent of cartels.

The Nonprimary Sector

The nonprimary sector, as we observed earlier, can be divided into import-substitution–oriented, export type, and services. We concentrate here largely on the first two. For our purposes, we must keep in mind that in the case of restrictive business practices affecting import substitution activities, the immediate impact is on the domestic market. Such practices may also affect import activities, given that developing countries are largely importers of technology and capital goods. In the case of export-oriented manufacturing activities, restrictions may relate to both imports and exports, but particularly to the latter. The domestic sector is also affected to the extent that exports will involve local production. The point is, of course, that the market outlets are mainly overseas. The available data often fail to make this qualitative distinction, so that often one is not in a position to identify the precise extent to which these sectors are involved in restrictive business practices agreements. Against this, it must be remembered that research work on the restrictive business practices of transnationals in developing countries is still of a largely preliminary nature. Most of the research, however, seems to relate largely to export-oriented type of activities.[54]

A case of the import-substitution type of restrictive business practices is to be found in the recent experience of the Brazilian electrical industry. In 1950, as a result of the growing domestic market for electrical equipment, local production by Brazilian manufacturers was actively encouraged. Production was concentrated on transmission equipment and household appliances. By the mid 1960s, a number of transnational corporations, such as AEG, ASEA, Brown Boveri, Ercole Marelli, General Electric, Hitachi, Siemens, Toshiba, and ACEC-Charleroi, entered the local market. By 1972 transnational corporations controlled 78 percent of the market, and by 1976 the share of transnationals in the local market was estimated at 90 percent.[55]

Before 1960, members of the International Electrical Association (an international cartel) considered Brazil as an export market. To it, the cartel assigned particular transnationals. Together, these transnationals fixed prices for the sale of electrical goods to the Brazilian market. When transnationals began producing in the local market, the tradition of collusive agreements was continued and regular meetings among them were reported in Brazil. The main idea was to limit price competition and to consolidate market power among the transnationals.[56]

The two main techniques adopted by transnationals to control the Brazilian market were (1) control over materials and components that local manufacturers needed, and (2) use of import regulations and concessions. The local manufacturers depended on members of the international cartel for ancillary and test equipment, as well as components, including insulators used for transformers and circuit breakers. In the former case of control, evidence suggests that the control of materials and components was used to weaken local competition by withholding components completely or by creating harmful instability in terms of material supplies. Second, import regulations in Brazil allowed for preferential treatment to be granted to essential capital equipment obtained from abroad if the equipment differed in price or delivery terms, as well as in technical specifications, from domestic products.

Under these circumstances, transnationals were able to use the provisions of the import regulations to manipulate prices for vital imports (supplied by parent companies)—namely, through price cutting—to the detriment of local competition.[57] This manipulation operated to prevent the local development of materials and component industries in the electrical equipment sector.[58] Thus, local manufacturers not members of the collusive agreements involving the respective transnationals "were weakened financially and either they were taken over by cartel members or they went bank-rupt.''[59] In this way, by eliminating the weak firms, the transnationals con-solidated their strength in the domestic market. This experience would seem instructive for policymakers and economists concerned with optimizing in-fant-industry possibilities in developing countries. Most studies on the pro-motion of infant industries almost invariably ignore the role of restrictive business practices in industrial development policies pertaining thereto. Yet, it is a consideration that in many respects appears quite pertinent.

A similar pattern of the use of restrictive business practices in the electri-cal industry and in ownership concentration by transnationals has been re-corded by Newfarmer for Mexico, Argentina, and Peru.[60] This study found that takeovers have played a major role in the process of monopolization of the electrical sector. Thus, Newfarmer argues, "The acquisition activity of transnational corporations throughout the world has been formidable in the electrical industry."[61] This may indeed be so, but it is only more so com-pared to other activities in which transnationals have been engaged. The point is that acquisitions seem to be a popular strategy by transnationals for market consolidation in quite a number of sectors. However, we are still discussing the electrical industry.

In Latin America, the average share of acquisitions by U.S. transna-tionals in overseas investment in the electrical sector was 42 percent between 1958 and 1968, and in some countries it was as high as 64 percent.[62] In the case of Africa and Asia especially, countries with small domestic markets, the process of acquisition has been less acute.[63] Most of the investment by transnationals in the electrical industry was regarded as defensive in char-acter, especially since import substitution tended to favor local produc-tion.[64] Therefore, the need was felt by such enterprises to protect export markets in developing countries by jumping tariff walls and producing lo-cally.

In this connection, some developing countries have rejected bids for elec-trical equipment, alleging price fixing by dominant transnationals operating worldwide. A case in point is Saudi Arabia. In 1977, it alleged that major transnationals "have agreed to fix the price of their bids to share in illegal profits."[65] The government also complained that transnationals had car-ried out price discrimination by setting prices for exports of electrical equip-ment to Saudi Arabia higher than those of other countries.[66]

Collusion in tendering is one of the more prominent features of restric-tive business practices of transnationals in the capital goods industry. A re-cent OECD report expressed concern over the rising importance of this form of restrictive business practices worldwide. While the OECD study failed to make specific reference to developing countries, the finding is especially relevant. For instance, remember that developing countries generally tend to lack a capital goods sector. The sale of these goods is totally in the hands of transnationals, and goods are often sold through tendering arrangements.

The OECD identified a number of restrictive business practices found in tendering that seem of relevance to developing countries. They include the following:

Cover bids whereby collusion is exercised to submit the lowest bid through tendering rings;
Give-and-take price practices in which the aim is to use dominant positions to charge as much as the traffic can bear;
Collusive tendering through a trade association whereby there is an agreement or constitution or other kinds of collaboration prior to the submission of tenders;
Joint tenders through which tenders are collectively submitted;
Common sales agencies;
Agreements not to compete in tendering.[67]

Evidence is further available in the pharmaceutical industry to provide another example of the widespread use of restrictive business practices in domestic markets in developing countries. The Philippine example is probably illustrative of similar experiences in a wide cross section of developing countries. In the 1950s the Philippine government imposed controls concerning the importation of foreign drugs. A number of transnationals, such as Muller and Phipps, Merck Sharp and Dohme, Abbott, Squibb, United Drug, Pfizer, Warner Chilcott, Winthrop-Sterling, and Roche, began local production to maintain their overseas market share. By 1970, only two Philippine companies ranked among the leading pharmaceutical manufacturers in the country. In terms of sales volume, transnationals had captured 70 percent of the local market.[68] In the words of a recent survey, "The industry is therefore dominated by foreign companies and their subsidiaries."[69] The bulk of pharmaceutical inputs are derived from foreign inputs supplied by the parent companies. In other words, local raw materials that had previously been featured as part of the indigenous industry are hardly used. Restrictive business practices used by transnationals to dominate the local market have included tied purchases of raw materials, export restrictions, and transfer-pricing strategies. Advertising and sales promotion have also played a role in diverting demand away from traditional drugs. Prices have often been found to be twenty times higher than the prices of similar drugs on some European markets.[70] Lall and others have found similar prices and sourcing strategies of transnationals engaged in the pharmaceutical industry in other developing countries.[71] A study on the restrictions of exports in foreign collaboration agreements in the Philippines and India has found a wide range of restrictive business practices affecting principal manufacturing activity, such as in the manufacture of food, beverages, textiles, electrical supplies, chemicals, metals, petroleum, tobacco products, and office equipment. In the case of the Philippines, the restriction on export products covered by licensing agreements was highest and covered 65 percent of the total number of agreements with restrictive clauses.[72] For example, export restrictions were 82 out of 126 restrictive agreements. Of these, 49 involved a total ban on exports, and 67 were tied purchases. The sample covered 254 agreements for the year 1970. See Table 5.2 for a complete breakdown.

Table 5.2. Types of Export Restrictive Clauses: Philippines, 1970

Type of Restrictive Clause	Number of Agreements with Restrictive Clauses
Export Restrictions	82
Global ban on exports	49
Exports prohibited to specified countries	4
Exports permitted to specified countries only	1
Prior approval for exports	17
Exports permitted to or through specified firms only	6
Restrictions on use of trademarks in exports	5
Other Restrictions	
Tied purchases	67
Restrictions on production pattern	5
Payment of minimum royalty	13
Improvements to licensor	14
Non-Philippines law to settle disputes	21
Restriction on termination	3
Total number of restrictive agreements[a]	126
Total number of agreements	254

Source: UNCTAD, Restrictive Business Practices (Geneva, 1971), p. 21.
[a]The total number of export restrictions and other restrictions can exceed the total number of agreements with restrictions because a given agreement can contain an export restriction as well as other types of restrictions. A given agreement can also contain one or more types of export restrictions.

Table 5.3.   Types of Export Restrictive Clauses: India, 1964–1969

Type of Restrictive Clause	*Number of Agreements with Restrictive Clauses*	
	Effective Agreements Approved up to March 1964[a]	*Effective Agreements Approved April 1964– March 1969*[b]
Export Restrictions	455	161
Global ban on exports	36	3
Exports prohibited to specified countries	42	60
Exports permitted to specified countries only	197	60
Prior approval for exports	149	15
Exports permitted to or through specified firms only	20	16
Restrictions on use of trademarks in exports	5	5
Other export restrictions	6	2
Other Restrictions		
Tied purchases	154	16
Restrictions on production pattern	65	—
Payment of minimum royalty	55	4
Restriction on sales procedures	18	1
Other restrictions	3	1
Total number of agreements with restrictive clauses[c]	527	171
Total number of effective agreements	1,051	342

Source: UNCTAD, *Restrictive Business Practices* (Geneva, 1971), p. 22.

[a]Figures in this column are based on Reserve Bank of India, *Foreign Collaboration in Indian Industry: Survey Report* (Bombay, Examiner Press, 1968), p. 106. The figures relate to agreements in force on April 1, 1961, or thereafter, covering all government approvals till March 1964.

[b]Figures in this column are preliminary and subject to revision. These relate to agreements that came into force after obtaining government approval between April 1964 and March 1969.

[c]The total of export restrictions and other restrictions can exceed the total number of agreements with restrictions because a given agreement can contain an export restriction as well as other types of restrictions. A given agreement can also contain one or more export restrictions.

A similar pattern was found for India before 1964 and between 1964 and 1969. For example, effective agreements up to March 1964 showed that over 50 percent of the agreements had restrictive clauses—specifically, 527 out of 1,051. Of these, 455 involved export restrictions, and 154 involved tied purchases. Between 1964 and 1969, out of 342 agreements examined, over 50 percent, or 171, were found to have had restrictions. Export restrictions numbered 167. See Table 5.3.

A similar picture emerges for Mexico. Table 5.4 shows that out of 126 restrictive clauses examined, 106 contained export restrictions.

An international survey was carried out in countries in which general information was available on restrictive business practices involving transnational corporations. This survey shows the predominance of export restrictions in the respective countries. Other practices, such as tied purchases and restrictions on production patterns, have also been common. The results are shown in Table 5.5.

In a study of 451 contracts involving operations of transnationals in Latin America—35 (Bolivia), 140 (Colombia), 175 (Chile), 12 (Ecuador), 89 (Peru)—Vaitsos identified the following practices that were widespread in

Table 5.4. Types of Export Restrictive Clauses: Mexico, 1969

Type of Restrictive Clause	Number of Agreements with Restrictive Clauses
Export Restrictions	106
Global ban on exports	53
Exports prohibited to specified countries	3
Exports permitted to specified countries only	1
Prior approval for exports	13
Price control on exports	4
Exports permitted to or through specified firms	12
Restrictions on use of trademarks in exports	15
Export quotas	5
Other Restrictions	
Tied purchases	1
Restrictions on production patterns	19
Total number of restrictive clauses	126
Total number of restrictive agreements	109

Source: UNCTAD, Restrictive Business Practices (Geneva, 1971), p. 22.

Table 5.5.   Types of Export Restrictions

Type of Restriction	Country
Export restrictions (general)[a]	Brazil, Chile, Colombia, El Salvador, Ghana, Guatemala, Honduras, India, Kuwait, Malta, Mexico, Pakistan, Philippines, Singapore
Global ban on exports	Brazil, Colombia, Guatemala, Kuwait, India, Mexico, Pakistan
Exports prohibited to specified countries	India, Mexico, Pakistan, Singapore
Exports permitted to specified countries only	Brazil, El Salvador, Guatemala, Honduras, India, Iran, Kuwait, Malta, Mexico
Prior approval for exports	India, Mexico, Pakistan, Philippines
Export quotas	Colombia, India, Mexico
Price control on exports	Colombia, India, Mexico, Pakistan
Exports restricted to specified products	Colombia, India
Exports permitted to or through specified firms only	Honduras, India
Exports of substitute products prohibited	Colombia, Philippines
Tied purchases	Brazil, Colombia, India, Philippines
Restrictions on production patterns	Colombia, India, Mexico, Philippines
Restrictions on disclosure	Brazil, India

Source: UNCTAD, Restrictive Business Practices (Geneva, 1971), p. 19.
[a]A few countries noted the existence of export restrictions in general terms with no specification as to type. These countries, plus those that specified the types of restrictions, are included in this category.

these countries: tied-in clauses for intermediate production processes, export-restrictive clauses, tied-in clauses relating to personnel, and sale and resale clauses. The sectors affected were pharmaceutical, rubber, chemical, and electronics. Vaitsos argued that through these clauses, high monopoly rents were reaped by transnationals.[73]

As a percentage of total restrictions, export restrictions were as follows: Bolivia, 77 percent; Chile, 72 percent; Colombia, 77 percent; Ecuador, 75 percent; and Peru, 89 percent. The sectoral distribution of these export restrictions was at the same time as follows: textiles, 88 percent; pharmaceuticals, 89 percent; chemicals, 78 percent; food and beverages, 73 percent; and others, 91 percent. One of the main reasons advanced for the use of these practices was the extension of exclusive monopoly privileges in relation to the importation of intermediate products.[74] The point is that restrictions stemmed from control that transnationals were able to exercise over patents and other forms of technology. We return to the question of technology shortly. It is also true, however, that another reason for restricting exports could be agreements among transnationals as to market-sharing arrangements.

Another area of restrictive business practices concerns the use of transfer pricing. Brief mention was made of this earlier. Empirical elaboration is now needed. A special feature of the price behavior of transnationals is the prices charged for intracorporate sales. We noted earlier the importance of intracorporate relations among transnationals in developing countries. This is relevant to the study of transnational activities in primary and nonprimary sectors, as well as in the service sectors. Most empirical work on the transfer pricing of transnationals seems to have been confined to the secondary sector. Transfer pricing can be used in principle to "strengthen the competitive position of the parent or subsidiary and to control competition in a given industry."[75] For instance, underpricing of intermediate products, raw materials, and services can be used, thus "enabling the receiving unit to lower prices either to increase its market share or to prevent entry of newcomers [predatory pricing]."[76] This would be a case of limit pricing, which was referred to earlier. Also, overpricing is a function of some exclusive monopoly rights and can be used to overcharge competitors or to evade taxes in a particular country since, all things being equal, higher input prices would mean fewer declared profits. Thus, this is consistent with maximizing profits for the corporate entity as a whole. Evidence exists as to the use of such practices in such sectors as transport equipment, nonelectrical machinery, and chemicals, including pharmaceuticals. For some countries, these sectors account for as much as 70 percent of total intracorporate trade.[77]

Research on the intracorporate pricing of transnationals is of recent origin. Most of the work has been done in Latin America. Even so, it seems indicative enough of trends elsewhere, yet to be researched. In Colombia, a government inquiry was set up to examine the role of transfer pricing of transnationals. The inquiry covered the following sectors: pharmaceuticals, rubber, chemicals, and electrical goods. Between 1967 and 1970, the weighted average of overpricing was set at 155 percent for pharmaceuticals; electrical goods, 54 percent; rubber, 44 percent; and chemicals, 25 percent.

Overpricing on some individual items, such as pharmaceuticals, was at times as high as 3,000 percent.[78] In the case of Chile, transfer pricing was reported in the pharmaceutical industry, affecting fifty products. On average overpricing was set at 100 percent.[79] In Peru, transfer pricing was found to affect twenty-two pharmaceutical firms and overpricing ranged from 5 to 300 percent of normal market prices. Likewise, in Ecuador an investigation covering six product groups found transfer pricing to be as high as 100 percent.[80] In the case of Iran during the late 1960s, average transfer pricing among chemical firms amounted to overcharging of up to 199 percent.[81] However, 50 percent of the cases involved overpricing from 200 to 999 percent.

In the Philippines, a report in *Business Asia* found overpricing to be significant. The article argued that transfer pricing was primarily responsible for transnational firms' earning as much as 1,000 percent on the price of finished drugs sold in the Philippines.[82] Data on India between 1970 and 1971 show that overpricing in the chemical sector ranged between 143 percent and 347 percent.[83] Studies on underpricing are relatively uncommon. Morgenstern and Mueller found underpricing to be widespread in Latin America, on an average, 40 percent.[84] Another area for which evidence is available concerning the use of restrictive business practices by transnational corporations is technology transfer. Here again, however, data are far from adequate. A recent study on licensing agreements (mainly patents and trademarks) between transnational firms and other firms in developing countries has revealed the following facts: In Argentina, out of 60 contracts, 28 percent had territorial restrictions; in Bolivia, out of 35 contracts, 83 percent had territorial restrictions and 83 percent limitations on purchase, output, and sale. In Chile, 175 contracts revealed that 96 percent had territorial restrictions; in Colombia, out of 117 contracts, 90 percent had territorial restrictions; in Ecuador, out of 12 contracts, 79 percent had territorial restrictions and 77 percent limitations on purchase, output, and sale. In Ethiopia, out of 7 contracts, 71 percent had territorial restrictions and 86 percent limitations on purchase, output, and sale. In India, 43 percent of contracts in foreign collaboration agreements examined had territorial restrictions, and other restrictions relating to purchase, output, and sale were prevalent. In Mexico, 97 percent of similar contracts had territorial restrictions; in Peru, 99 percent had territorial restrictions and 62 percent limitations on purchase, output, and sale; in the Philippines, 32 percent had territorial restrictions, 26 percent limitations on purchase, output, and sale, and 71 percent had financial provisions. Pakistan, Ghana, Kuwait, Singapore, and Malta are among other countries in which restrictions relating to the use of imported technology were also found to be important.[85]

In the Caribbean, an examination was made of 115 agreements (33 in Guyana and 82 in Trinidad), and a large number of cases involving the use of restrictive business practices were reported. No firm quantitative estimates have as yet been forthcoming.[86] The study covered a sample of local firms that had licensing agreements with transnationals. No comprehensive figures are available for Africa as such. However, a general study has identified the following practices found to be widespread: transfer pricing, market rigging, and restrictions in terms of personnel.[87] In the latter regard, the ILO has drawn attention to the employment practices of transnational corporations.[88]

The foregoing would suggest that territorial market and product allocation strategies are important considerations. Thus, it could be argued that the restrictive practices associated therewith may enable transnationals to maintain captive technology markets by tying the technology recipients to the supplier. In this sense, forced complementarity would seem to be a consequence. It should be noted that the restrictive business practices affecting technology transfer would seem not to involve collusion among transnationals in specific technological processes as such, but between parents and subsidiaries, affiliates, or joint ventures. One reason for this is the element of secrecy that characterizes particular technological processes. Even so, collusion can take place between distinct transnationals with regard to market divisions for particular technologies firmwise.

So far we have not dealt with cartels that affect transnationals in the manufacturing sector, although previously we looked at cartels in the primary sector. However, a study on cartels among major transnational corporations has identified a number of international cartel arrangements affecting developing countries—for example, pharmaceuticals, steam-generating and fuel-burning equipment, steel products, farm tractors, among others.[89]

Another area for which some evidence is available on the use of restrictive business practices concerns the transnational marketing groups referred to earlier. A recent study by the United Nations has identified three broad measures adopted by such corporations to use their market power to control marketing and distribution affecting the trade of developing countries.[90] In terms of arrangements for territorial allocation of markets and product takeovers, manipulation of prices has been identified as the main strategy. In terms of collective action by transnationals, it is argued that market power is reinforced by collective and cartel agreements with other firms. Also, marketing barriers to entry have been identified as an important consideration.

Product differentiation, advertising, promotion, after-sales service, and control over information have been identified as the main assets of such groups in their competitive efforts. However, precise data are lacking insofar as these strategies, and the effects of such strategies, by transnational marketing corporations go. Here there is no substitute for primary research. Certain other services, such as banking, are also not removed from attempts by transnational firms at market control. Banking in developing countries has been a long-established domain of transnational corporations. Little research has been done on the role of restrictive business practices in this area. In the case of the Caribbean, we have elsewhere documented the relevance of such practices to transnational banks.[91]

In conclusion, certain observations on the data so far reviewed are in order. The data are of a very preliminary nature. In the first place, they do not cover all transnationals operating in oligopolistic-type markets, nor are they fully adequate for intercountry comparisons. Some countries, notably in Latin America, are subjected to more research than others, such as those in Africa. Also, data hardly exist for a large number of countries. Further, the data relate to different time periods and do not cover all sectors. For instance, the service sector seems to have been hardly researched. Moreover, the data do not show trends in countries or sectors so that one is not armed with enough hard evidence to detect whether such practices have been increasing over the years and at what rates. Also, as mentioned earlier, the data often fail to make adequate distinctions between import-substitution–oriented activities and the export-processing type. Presumably, different strategic considerations will apply to each of these sectors. Also, the studies do not usually make special allowance for restrictive business practices as a dynamic strategic consideration by firms—namely, how they respond to changes in market and other considerations over time. However, in spite of these limitations, the evidence would seem to give a rough indication of the importance of the restrictive business practices of transnationals.

Further countrywide research will probably tend to be somewhat consistent with at least some of the evidence observed here. The contention that the market power of transnational corporations in developing countries "was often considerable and abuses of such power occurred"[92] is therefore not an unrealistic one.

6 DEVELOPMENT IMPLICATIONS OF RESTRICTIVE BUSINESS PRACTICES

One convenient way of dealing with the study of restrictive business practices and development is to consider the world economy in a two-sectoral sense. Assume, for instance, that there is a restrictive business practices intensive sector that is broadly called developing countries. The reasons why this can be called a restrictive business practices intensive sector have already been discussed—namely, the nature of the markets in which transnational corporations are found, the reliance of developing countries on such corporations for trade and production, and the absence of adequate controls for dealing with such practices. Developed countries, however, usually have controls for regulating restrictive business practices. Therefore, in all probability the developing-countries sector is likely to have a higher incidence of such practices than is the developed-countries sector. We are in no position to establish the precise extent of this. Developed countries cannot be regarded as a nonrestrictive business practices sector, however. The reason for this is that although such practices are controlled, they are not completely eliminated.

Another explicit assumption is called for here, relating to the alternative position regarding the competitive process in developing countries, if one assumes that transnational corporations now active directly and indirectly in such economies do not exist. Developing countries are often pictured as static economies. However, reason suggests that we must abandon static assumptions for our purpose. We have seen the importance of dynamic considerations to the competitive process involving firms from developed capitalist countries. In like manner, we may regard the indigenous market structures of developing countries to exhibit dynamic features of their own, though to a lesser extent than those in developed countries. Such features are likely to reveal themselves in the emergence of new firms, the decline of others, the introduction of new products, and changes in the use of technology, among other things, over time.[1] However, it is difficult to speculate as to the extent of these features, even though they would seem more likely to be more prominent in growth-oriented developing countries than in others.

SOME NEGATIVE ASPECTS

Rural Development

We saw in Chapter 5 the role of plantations in the economic life of a large number of developing countries. Much discussion has taken place of late on aspects of rural development, such as maldistribution of land, the associated problem of unequal distribution of incomes, and the problem of poverty.[2] For example, there is a growing school of economists that argues that the most central feature of underdevelopment is to be found in the rural political economy of developing countries.[3] Our own view on the matter does not seem to be important. It is enough to note the importance of the rural sector to development. Several factors account for problems of maldevelopment in rural areas of the Third World. One that seems to have escaped much attention, however, is that of restrictive business practices. The relevance of restrictive business practices of transnationals to rural development stems from the fact that through these practices, transnationals, as we saw, have been able to monopolize large holdings of land (often the more productive ones) and that this, it could be reasoned, has deprived other socioeconomic groups from having access to comparable resources. They have also been able to hold monopolistic conditions in the labor markets in developing countries, thus enabling them to influence the determination of rural wage rates and conditions of work to an important extent. This is so even though wage rates offered by plantations tend to be higher than those offered by local enterprises. However, wage setting is not removed from other considerations, such as organized unions existing in the plantation sector in order to increase the bargaining position of workers vis à vis such enterprises. It is true that the dominance of plantations has declined over the years, but these observations would nevertheless appear relevant since they go some way toward explaining some of the unequal socioeconomic results that have been historically determined as a result of economic control by transnationals.

In this regard, it should be noted that plantations had access not only to land but also to other key agricultural inputs, such as irrigation, credit, means of transport, and command over processing facilities. What the possible impact of these inputs on the present conditions of poverty and dispossession in rural areas is has yet to be assessed. Several writers on rural poverty have attributed this condition partly to the workings of transnationals engaged in the plantation sector. If this is so, and if it is accepted that restrictive business practices have been an important corporate strategy of plantations in developing countries, then it seems that such practices might have played a powerful role in determining rural poverty. Some evidence from the Caribbean seems partly to support this, though other examples can be found.

Natural Resource Development

The question of ownership and control of natural resources has been a feature of recent resolutions passed by the United Nations. It is also a key feature of the so-called New International Economic Order.[5] The common view taken is that foreign ownership of strategic and/or nonrenewable resources may operate against long-term national-development objectives of developing countries. This view is partly confirmed by studies on bauxite and copper, for example, in which some evidence has suggested that very limiting processing took place, high profits were repatriated, and the overall contribution to development was extremely limited.[6] The point is that the operations of many transnational mining companies are likely to be detrimental to the development of competing indigenous industries for reasons alluded to earlier. Reference was already made to tin in Malaysia, for example. It is true that such transnationals bring in the latest technology and systems of operation in exploration and refining that tend to make them enjoy competitive advantages over local firms. It could be argued that control over such key resources by a few firms has enabled such firms to dictate the rules of the game not only in terms of competition but also over rewards and concessions from governments. If this is so, restrictive business practices would seem to have a crucial role to play not only in the process of monopolization of these firms but also in the power this process confers on the respective firms. It is true that productivity would tend to be higher than in competitive local firms using old technology, for instance. However, this does not interfere with the validity of the point.

Output

It is commonly held that by restricting output, an oligopolist or collusive monopoly is able to maximize profits. This is likely, all things being equal, to reduce economic growth and therefore to affect the well-being of developing countries. Both growth and well-being are critical issues in development—growth in real output is necessary to relieve absolute poverty levels in such countries. While growth is not a sufficient condition for development, it surely is a necessary condition. Hence, limitation on output, a common form of restrictive business practices as we saw earlier, would seem likely to reduce the bundle of goods and services potentially available to a given economy. This assumes that production is locally geared, which need not be the case.

Employment

Often the discussion of the modern sector in developing countries makes reference to the capital-intensive techniques of production contributing to technological unemployment in such countries. The argument is that developing countries have a surplus supply of labor—hence, the relevance of a technique that maximizes the use of its abundant supplies of labor. It is possible to argue that the role of restrictive business practices is relevant here to the question of unemployment and development (although it is hardly accepted as such). For example, as we saw previously, a common feature of restrictive business practices may be the reduction of output (in this case, both for the domestic market and for exports). Under this assumption, it could be argued that labor intake by firms is likely to be less than in more competitive conditions. If this is so, then the employment boundary within given production techniques is not extended to the fullest possible extent. The real extent of this could only be established as a result of in-depth research into the labor-absorptive patterns of particular enterprises. The extent to which labor is not fully utilized here would certainly differ depending on the choice of techniques applied. For instance, the more labor-intensive the techniques, the greater would seem the possibility of adding more labor to the optimum limit possible with this technique; conversely, the more capital-intensive the process, the more likely that labor contribution to additional output ranges possible—let us say, under fully competitive conditions—will be less than in the former case. At any rate, the principle of the argument still holds—namely, that employment suffers.

Further, we saw that restrictive business practices may limit the employment creation of certain key skills locally. It may be part of the strategy of firms, for example, to limit access of knowledge and strategic employment posts, such as in management, finance, and forms of engineering activity, to overseas personnel whose loyalty to company secrets and so forth might not be brought into question. This strategy may be relevant for such high-technology industries as chemicals and electronics. Whatever the reasons for this restriction, clearly such skills are vital to the development process of developing countries. The shortage of skills, as we saw in Chapter 2, has long been identified as a crucial factor in development. Thus, it could be said that such restrictive policy operates to limit human capital formation in developing countries. It is not surprising, therefore, that the ILO in a recent resolution called on transnationals to adopt a more positive attitude toward offering employment opportunities to nationals of developing countries in such key areas.[7]

Income Distribution

We alluded to income distribution earlier. Elaboration is now needed in the context of developing countries. The point of the argument is that allowing firms to monopolize markets also allows them to obtain a disproportionately large amount of income derived from profits. Theory suggests that the excess profits are brought about because of the absence of competition. Firms are therefore able to charge higher than normal prices for products or services, and as a result they are able to earn supernormal profits.[8] This is especially so if one assumes away the existence of progressive tax rates. This would seem to be so at least in a large number of cases given, for instance, the need of developing countries to attract foreign capital—thus, the need to create a suitable business climate. Political stability is certainly important, as is the ability of firms to earn high profits. Income distribution could therefore be affected at the following levels: between foreign-market–dominating enterprises vis à vis smaller local producers in the same market, as well as in other markets, and between foreign firms vis à vis wage earners and other groups. Recall that we have already drawn attention to the weak competitive position of local firms vis à vis market-dominating enterprises. This may be the result of several factors, but profits may be one of them, especially if it is argued that local firms tend to be of the infant-industry type, meaning that they have not yet fully matured and so cannot reap high rewards from competition as well-established foreign firms.

However, it is true that some studies, by the ILO, for example, have pointed to the fact that foreign firms tend to pay higher wages than do local firms in similar industries. However relevant this point may be, it does not affect the argument within the foreign-market–dominating sector, especially if profit rates are exceptionally high. It does, however, mean that in terms of wage-earning groups, an element of inequality of incomes is introduced. On the one hand, this may be a positive element for the wage earners concerned. On the other hand, it also could very well be the result of a predatory attempt by such firms to obtain sufficient local labor even if it means destroying local firms. Even if it is not predatory as such, payment of higher than market wages can operate to increase local wages above the level that smaller local firms may be able to pay if they are to stay in business.

Studies on profitability levels between transnational firms and local firms operating in the same markets in developing countries are sadly lacking, and more in-depth research is required to establish in a concrete manner the above speculations or to refute them. However, some studies have produced evidence on the monopoly earning capacities of market-dominating transnational firms in developing countries[9]—for example, prices, ability to control markets, and so on.

Resource Misallocation

Closely related to some of the points already raised is the question of resource misallocation. The standard theories on industrial organization and corporate performance, as we saw in Chapter 1, lead to the conclusion that restrictive business practices result in lower economic efficiency than would occur in a situation in which competition was prevailing. In this regard, the definition of the optimum situation to be achieved under highly competitive conditions is worth recalling. Production will be at the lowest unit costs, and prices will be as low as is consistent with covering costs and allowing for a small margin of profit. Goods will be produced at the most efficient level of production, and all economic resources will be used to their best possible advantages.

We have noted the role of restrictive business practices, for example, in output, profits, and employment in developing countries. Sales tied to import sources (which we saw was a widespread practice among transnationals), it may be argued, tend to prohibit the development of local inputs and resources. As is shown in Chapter 7, several international resolutions on restrictive business practices have urged transnationals to adopt a more host-country–oriented resource-sourcing pattern. The adoption of foreign input sourcing of transnationals would appear to be most frequent in vertically integrated enterprises, especially those engaged in assembly-type operations—hence, the high degree of intrafirm trade often found here. The full utilization of local resources would seem vital to enhance the economic development possibilities in low-income countries. This is so because it could render the structure of production more heterogeneous by spreading economic activity cross-sectorally via various forms of linkages. Most developing countries, as noted earlier, were to a large extent primary producers and lacked diversity in the structure of domestic production. Local resource utilization—raw materials, intermediate products, and forms of processing linked to primary production—could provide an important ingredient to future industrial development efforts in developing countries, as the African, Caribbean, and Pacific Group of countries associated with the European Economic Community under the Lome Convention has so often argued.[10]

Welfare Effects of Prices

Consider the case of collusive and other forms of price fixing by transnational firms in domestic markets in developing countries, a frequent feature of restrictive business practices among such firms. The macroeconomic effects will vary depending on the relative importance of the firms in question to the respective economies and how widespread the practice is. However, it can be said that such prices will mean that consumers, all things being equal, will have to pay more than normal for the goods being sold. We saw already the low prevailing levels of real incomes in developing countries. Some of the goods affected might be those necessary for the satisfaction of basic needs, which means that an unduly heavy burden of prices in the form of quasi-monopoly rents will have to be paid by the poor. A case in point is the pharmaceutical sector, in which, as we saw, prices have been found to be extraordinarily high in some cases because of the abuse of dominant market power. At the same time, Lall and others have found that the prices for generic products (namely, products with identical chemical characteristics) sold elsewhere, but under competitive conditions, have been much lower.[11] Given the social need for pharmaceutical products in poor societies, in which the incidence of disease and ill health is likely to be high, it could be said that the pricing behavior of firms in these circumstances is a negative factor working against improvement in the quality of life. However, consumers may benefit from the limit-pricing strategies of such firms, but probably only in a short-term way. Once the market position is assured, the likelihood is that prices will be manipulated in such a manner as to create conditions of abnormal profit-earning possibilities.

The same conditions may apply to less essential goods that are produced for local consumption under import-substituting inducements, negatively affecting the growth of real incomes. Schumpeter himself, a protagonist of large-scale firms, concedes that restrictive business practices could tend to operate to the disadvantage of consumers.[12]

Our point is that, on the one hand, this problem is likely to be more acute in poor countries, since buyers will tend to be relatively poor, with a great many absolutely poor. On the other hand, prices for high- and middle-income goods will tend to shift the resources of potential savers (given that local savings are usually derived from these income-earning groups—the propensity to save here being greater than that of lower-income earners), all things being equal, away from the local economy into the hands of transnational producers. Thus, if profits are repatriated—a situation that is more often encountered than not—it would seem to follow that the local savings and investment potential are being dried up. Savings are noted to be in short supply in most developing countries. Lack of savings would mean that local investors are unable to finance their investment projects. However, the luxury-goods market in some developing countries may be quite small. At the same time, in quite a number of countries, growing middle classes brought about by rapid social and economic changes constitute an important market.

It remains true, though, that transnational firms may bring with them capital and other resources from abroad that may benefit domestic investment. The point is, however, if we assumed the nonexistence of restrictive business practices or some control over these, abusive pricing practices may be less widespread. This would in turn allow for greater domestic savings and greater aggregate domestic investment on the further assumption that entrepreneurial talent is forthcoming.

Effects on Local Competition

The point regarding the effects of local competition was referred to earlier in a slightly different context. If it is argued, for example, that restrictive business practices of transnational corporations tend to operate in a manner that stifles local competition, a number of consequences would seem to follow. In this light, we saw the role of acquisitions of local firms by transnationals in an effort, among other things, to penetrate local markets. The reduction of local firms from the domestic market will tend to create a situation in which dependency on transnationals is brought about and is indeed perpetuated. We noted in Chapter 2 that there was some criticism against undue reliance on transnationals in the economic life of developing countries. Suffice it to point out that more often than not the main decisions of transnational corporations tend to be taken in the parent headquarters.

The overriding consideration is not how these decisions fit into the social and developmental objectives of the host country, but how they relate to private corporate goals—hence, the possible divergence between the objectives of such firms and the societies in which they operate abroad.[13] The divergence between private interests and social ones has been a long-standing feature of welfare economics. Restrictive business practices that help to induce such a situation add a further dimension to this problem.

Further, it is sometimes held that the lack of local entrepreneurial talent is a major factor inhibiting the development process in developing countries. The point is, as some economists argue, that dynamic enterprise is vital to economic transformation. It is true that transnationals may fill some gap here. If it is argued that the restrictive business practices of transnationals tend to limit the potential dynamism of local firms (by stifling competition, for example), then in this vein it could be argued that such practices at the same time limit the role that local enterprise can be expected to play in economic transformation.

In light of this discussion, the notion of collective self-reliance among developing countries, which is a feature of the New International Economic Order already referred to, would appear to be equally relevant. Taking this position, the argument is that the development initiative must come from the developing countries themselves. The rationale behind this would seem to be that earlier periods of development were characterized by political relationships that allowed for decision making to be taken by colonial powers and that were not necessarily in the best long-term interests of the developing countries. Further, it is important that since development involves the satisfaction of human needs as well as the mobilization of human resources, people should be allowed to participate as fully as possible in this process.[14] This position is sometimes objected to on the grounds that proper decisions involve the use of technical wisdom that may be limited in many developing countries.

Technology

We have already seen the widespread use of restrictive business practices in technology-transfer transactions involving transnational enterprises. Though the sample was confined to a select group of developing countries, the indications are that these practices are a common feature of technology-transfer transactions between transnationals and developing countries.[15]

Within recent times, the question of the lack of a technological capability has come to be regarded as a major feature of underdevelopment.[16] Such capability is loosely defined in terms of the ability of an economy to generate indigenous technology and to adapt and absorb foreign technology. A quantitative definition is still lacking. However, the argument is that because of the lack of such a capability, developing countries, for one reason or another, have to rely upon imported capital-intensive technology that is far from optimal in terms of resource use and direct and indirect costs.[17]

The precise role of restrictive business practices in terms of the lack of a technological capability in developing countries is yet to be fully analyzed. However, it is evident that by tying local producers to imported technology, the restrictive business practices of transnationals engaged in technology transfer transactions tend to stultify the local market prospects for indigenous technology and for the modification of foreign technology to satisfy the factor mix in such countries. In other words, this amounts to freezing the market prospects for domestic technology. Also, tying local technology users to foreign suppliers prevents the search for alternative technology from abroad that might be cheaper and also more appropriate in terms of factor combinations. In this regard, attention is now being addressed to the reform of patent laws by some international organizations so as to increase the scope for developing countries to generate their own technology and to have easier access to available technology in the world market.[18]

These illustrations were meant to highlight the internal aspects of development associated with restrictive business practices. We now focus on the trading aspect of the problem.

IMPORTS

Several implications arise as regards imports. Some of the main ones are described in the following sections.

Prices of Goods in the Open Market

If markets are dominated by oligopolistic forces from the sellers' point of view, the question of arbitrarily inflated prices, often said to be a feature of such markets, becomes relevant. In other words, developing countries may have to pay higher than normal competitive prices for imported goods. This is also likely to apply to developed countries to some extent. It could be argued that developed countries are both importers and exporters of goods determined by such a market structure, so that there is countervailing power, as it were, on the export side. This situation is not strictly relevant to developing countries. Recall the relatively favorable terms of trade of goods imported by developing countries from developed ones. We are not sure of the precise extent of the influence of restrictive business practices of transnationals in this, but evidence suggests that they are likely to be important for reasons already alluded to—notably the market forces and the lack of legal control over corporate pricing behavior. The element of price rigidity, as we saw earlier, has often been cited as an oligopolistic behavior pattern.[19] Rigid prices could mean that in conditions of economic depression when prices are generally falling, they are relatively high instead (falling not as fast as other prices). However, in inflationary situations when prices are generally rising fast, rigid prices may not rise as fast, so that there may be some gain on the part of developing countries. It is possible, however, for price leadership behavior among oligopolies to take account of this by increasing prices when market conditions so dictate. The same would apply to depressions.[20] In this connection, it should be noted that importers from developing countries are often small-scale buyers and are therefore unable to exercise much power in terms of neutralizing price trends dictated by big international firms. This situation has led some researchers to advocate the promotion of bilateral monopolies (in this case, import pooling on the part of developing countries) so as to reduce possible international price distortions as they affect such countries' imports.[21] Remember that transnationals often have economic power much greater than that of many developing countries.

Further, against this background, one must recognize the foreign exchange difficulties facing developing countries. What this would seem to mean is that if prices are not determined by the free forces of demand and supply, developing countries may be taxed far beyond what their resources may permit in terms of prices for imported goods. It would seem that the international trade theory should pay more attention to the phenomenon of restrictive business practices as powerful economic agents on international prices. In this way, greater light could be shed on the matter.

Lack of Possibility to Explore Other Markets

We saw in Chapter 4 that developing countries were dependent on transnational corporations of selected developed countries for the bulk of their import requirements. If we assume that restrictions tend to tie such countries to transnationals engaged in import supplies, it clearly narrows the market range of such countries' imports. We made reference to this point earlier in terms of technological capability in developing countries. The point here is that some imports are frozen in alternative overseas markets, including socialist and other developing countries that offer better market prices. Given the scarce foreign exchange problems referred to previously, prospects for foreign exchange savings are limited, as is increased consumer welfare, which could be brought about as a result of lower real import prices. This would appear unfortunate in view of the high levels of poverty prevailing in such countries.

Import Dependency

Related to the last section is the question of import dependency on a few suppliers. While it is possibly a good thing to have secure import sources, it is sometimes argued that import dependency on limited sources can inhibit economic diversification and help to reinforce existing patterns of international division of labor between primary producers and nonprimary producers. The essence of this argument is as follows: The existing pattern of the world division of labor has been shaped to a large extent as a result of colonial economic relationships. Developing countries were needed to supply primary products for manufacture in metropolitan countries. In turn, they received their manufactured goods from metropolitan countries. As we have already seen, these are supplied largely by transnationals. If economic development is interpreted as a progressive transformation of economic structures into more complex and heterogeneous ones capable of producing a wide range of goods for internal demand, then it could be argued that import dependency of the type fostered by restrictive business practices limits economic development for the following reasons:

Production of goods manufactured, including parts and components, competing with imports from established sources is discouraged. When such production takes place, it is often associated with foreign technology and control so that little "learning by doing" is transferred to the local economy as such. True, the main body of persons employed are indigenous, but they are not necessarily engaged in key management, engineering, and technical positions that would allow them to master such technology.

In other words, the "tricks" of the game of production do not filter through to the economy. Thus the argument is that if developing countries are to develop, they first have to break this circle of dependency so that the indigenous resource base can be more fully tapped.[22]

One of the consequences sometimes associated with this relationship is forced obsolescence. One study has concluded that because of the dependence on the monopoly power of transnationals for goods, the "emphasis may be on replacement of goods rather than importing spare parts for repair."[23] However, this could be interpreted as merely a crisis of dependency of the type just discussed.

Transfer Pricing

The evidence on the effects of transfer pricing in developing countries is far from conclusive, if only because research in the area is still relatively new.[24] We have already seen the importance of intrafirm transactions. If higher than market prices are charged for imported goods, in principle this would be the same as a foreign exchange drainage on the importing country.

Research has also identified transfer pricing as a way of evading taxes.[25] Moreover, such transfer prices may be applied to local firms (either joint ventures with transnationals or independent enterprises having special links with transnationals) and may serve to limit the competitiveness of such firms to the extent that higher unit input prices are involved. Transfer prices may also be set below market prices. In this case, they can serve as limit pricing to keep out local competitors by predatory-pricing tactics. Either way, transfer pricing gives cause for some concern. Most recent attempts at controlling transnational corporations have, as Chapter 7 shows, drawn special attention to controlling this aspect of such corporations.

Balance-of-Payments Effects

From the foregoing points, the balance-of-payments effects clearly are of particular importance to the analysis of restrictive business practices—for instance, high import prices, replacement of products rather than repair, and tying import supplies. These considerations are likely to exert pressure on balance-of-payments problems in developing countries. An analysis of the balance-of-payments effects will have to take account of the export side as well, if exports are involved.

The role of transnationals in aggravating balance-of-payments problems in developing countries has been recognized for some time now, but little work has been done to examine the role of restrictive business practices in this. A study by Lall and Streeten has pointed to the adverse balance-of-payments effects of transnationals to a group of developing countries, largely in the Caribbean, Asia, and Africa.[26] Such effects likely were aggravated by restrictive business practices, especially on the import side given the sourcing patterns of the transnationals involved. Further, high rates of repatriation of profits, royalties, and fees, for example, may be a function of restrictive business practices that, by enforcing forms of collective monopoly behavior, have enabled profits, royalties, and fees to be high in the first place. This is not an idle point, given the role of prices in enabling firms to earn high profits, and, as we saw earlier, restrictive business practices seem quite acute in the case of technology-transfer relationships.

On the export side of the balance-of-payments equation, the limitation of exports may inhibit the foreign exchange earning capacity of an economy. We have already recognized the importance of such limitations in a number of arrangements involving the operations of transnational corporations in developing countries.

Aspects of Capital Procurement

It was noted earlier that collusive tendering has not been unknown in the history of restrictive business practices in developing countries. Tendering often applies to capital goods needed by developing countries for development projects. Restrictive business practices arrangements in tendering can have effects on the prices that such countries must pay to obtain such equipment, as well as on the terms under which it is sold, such as services, use of spare parts, and so on. However, limited research has been done in the area of restrictive business practices in tendering. It should be noted that tendering is fast becoming an important means through which the public sector in developing countries obtains capital goods. In this context, we have already referred to the importance of transnationals in the supply of such goods imported by developing countries.

EXPORTS

We already noted the importance of export limitation in terms of balance-of-payments considerations. It is now necessary to look at the question from a slightly different angle. It is widely recognized that developing countries need to diversify and expand their exports as a means of accelerating their development. This is especially so in the case of small-scale economies with limited internal markets. This export-led growth thesis is widely propagated by the UN resolution on a New International Economic Order, the Manila Declaration by developing countries in 1976, UNCTAD IV, and the Lome Convention between the African, Caribbean, and Pacific states and the EEC.[27] In this light, several studies on the contribution of transnational corporations to the manufactured exports of developing countries have pointed to the minor contributions made by such corporations in this area. Most of these exports, as we saw in Chapter 4, are confined to export-processing zones or assembly-type operations.

An OECD expert group has noted that the restrictive business practices activities of transnational corporations may be harmful to the export prospects of developing countries when they compete in similar international markets. The group noted the following in relation to transnational corporations engaged in export cartels:

> Firstly, export cartels may affect the price and supply of inputs used in exporting industries of developing countries by discriminatory practices and by refusal to sell certain materials or equipment to developing countries. Secondly, export cartels of enterprises may engage in monopolistic practices against their less-powerful competitors in developing countries. Thirdly, export interests of developing countries may be adversely affected by international market allocations binding also subsidiaries of cartel members in developing countries concerned.[28]

Another point relates to the freezing of alternative export outlets. For example, if channels of marketing and distribution are controlled by transnationals, restrictive business practices may be easily resorted to, thereby affecting developing countries' exports. Within vertically integrated firms, such as plantations and mining enterprises, transnationals often have their own marketing and distribution networks, as we already saw. Also, reference was made to transnational marketing groups that may operate independently of transnationals engaged in production. A recent experience may best serve to illustrate this point. When bauxite was nationalized in Guyana, the nationally owned firm sought to continue exports to the traditional North American market where the bauxite was normally sent for further processing. As a result of the nationalization, however, some of the North American bauxite markets were frozen, and alternative markets, notably in the Economic Council of Mutual Aid (COMECON) region, had to be sought. This practice has been widely documented in terms of product allocation arrangements by transnationals and in terms of the retaliatory behavior of such corporations to protect their own interests. The freezing of market outlets has also been documented. The case of the EEC illustrates what we have in mind. A recent case involved the Sporting Goods Fair arrangement, in which the specialized fair for winter sports goods admitted only those producers who sold their products exclusively to specialized dealers.[29] In this way, competing products were discriminated against and therefore lacked normal market outlets.

Export limitation may also operate to hinder intradeveloping country trade prospects. Often, in debates concerning international development strategy, the term *delinking* has been used to emphasize the need to foster forms of intra-Third World economic relationships. Prospects have been identified for manufactured exports as well as trade in some areas of technology.[30] Thus, it can be said that export limitation to the extent that it prevents such trade may operate to discourage this objective, though of course it could be argued that it is probably more politically motivated than economically justified. However, it could be countered that most economic policies have some political justification.

One needs to look more closely into export limitation, as the full extent to which this limitation represents a bias in terms of intra-Third World trade and other forms of economic relationships is not apparent from the available evidence.

A SUMMARY OF DEVELOPMENT IMPLICATIONS

The points made in this discussion are by no means fully comprehensive. However, they point to the negative aspects of restrictive business practices in developing countries.

The consequences will no doubt vary from country to country depending on the nature of trade and production relationships with transnationals, the precise nature of the markets and the degree of monopoly power associated with respective transnationals, and the measures that respective developing countries adopt for encouraging transnationals and for regulating their activities. For example, in situations in which transnationals are active mainly in primary production, such as in areas of agriculture, the rural development aspects of such consequences may be greater than if export-processing zone type of manufacture represents the main activity of transnationals. Further, import-substitution type of industrialization is likely to pose different consequences to the export-promotion type. Also, the extent to which individual countries depend on transnationals for trade—namely, imports and exports—is by no means uniform. In some countries, such as in the Caribbean, export agencies have begun to take over the role of international marketing of primary products. In other countries, such as Taiwan, the Philippines, and Singapore, export activities are largely in the hands of transnationals. On the import side, the difference in terms of effect is likely to depend in part on the extent to which intrafirm and arms-length sales are prevalent. As we saw, intrafirm imports are largely a function of the existence of transnationals in production activities in respective developing countries. On the one hand, some countries depend more heavily on transnationals for their industrial development than do others; the degree of reliance again is by no means uniform. Arms-length sales, on the other hand, will depend on the extent to which individual countries are affected by imports and exports generated by transnationals—in other words, the degree of "transnationalization" of their trade structures. Some developing countries, such as Guyana, Jamaica, Tanzania, Algeria, and Mozambique, are showing increasing trends toward import relations with COMECON countries. The effect of transnationals here is likely to be less than in other countries that depend on such corporations for their supply of goods.

Further, it is true that some individual developing countries may gain at the expense of others as a result of specific forms of restrictive business practices. For example, it may be argued that some practices enable transnational firms to have secure long-term market prospects as a result of consolidated market power. To the extent that such firms operate in particular developing countries, it could be said that such countries may benefit to some extent from this consolidation. This is likely to be true particularly if such firms are engaged in export activity where local competitive resources may be lacking. However, it remains true that social welfare for such countries as a group will tend to be lower than otherwise, all things being equal.

OTHER RELATED ASPECTS

An attempt to situate the concept of restrictive business practices of trans-national corporations in development is somewhat incomplete without reference to some of the benefits associated with the operation of such firms. We deal with some of those benefits found in the literature in the following sections.

Exports

While it is true that export limitation is a feature of a number of restrictive business practices operating in developing countries, it is also true that transnationals are involved in export promotion activities in developing countries, such as in the case of export-processing zone activities and in the area of primary production.

Such corporations tend to have a comparative advantage in export-oriented activities, given their worldwide marketing, communication, management, and distribution networks. That these corporations do not export as much as one would like them to is another matter. Evidence suggests that a large number of developing countries in Asia, the Caribbean, and Latin America have come to recognize the potential importance of transnationals in terms of market access to developed countries. There is also growing international recognition of this role of transnationals.[31] The point is, however, that exports are likely to be greater in the absence of such practices.

Employment

Data on the global employment impact of transnational corporations in developing countries are nonexistent. However, employment creation effects are clearly associated with such firms in their operations. This is so, even though it could be argued that "the employment contribution of foreign affiliates is small in relation to the massive employment problem."[32] In some countries, there is cause for concern. For example, in 1960, despite the overriding importance of oil and copper to the economies of Venezuela and Chile, employment generated by transnationals in these sectors was estimated at 2.3 percent and 4.1 percent, respectively, of the total labor force.[33] Also, there was little growth in employment in the extractive sector in these countries over the years.[34]

In Africa and the Caribbean, similar concern exists over the poor employment prospects of transnational corporations, especially in the manufacturing and extractive sectors. In plantation agriculture, labor is often used more abundantly, and the cause for concern is accordingly less. The point that employment created by transnationals is less than if more appropriate factor mixes were used by them, if potential linkages in developing economies were fully developed, or if restrictive business practices were nonexistent does not affect the principle of the argument.

Technology and Skills

It is sometimes argued that one of the chief advantages of transnational firms is that they introduce developing countries to a modern technological culture. In this way, according to this position, they fill certain resource gaps that are badly lacking in developing countries. For example, a characteristic feature of economic underdevelopment is the lack of up-to-date techniques of production and organization. Evidence seems to support this point to some extent, especially if one follows the product-cycle or technological-gap hypothesis to the logical conclusion. As we have already seen, such technology is not without negative implications, but these do not concern us presently. A recent study recognized that transnationals are "unique in providing from a single source a package of critical industrial inputs: capital, technology, managerial skills, and other services required for production and distribution."[35] In this light, it could be argued that developing countries are free to determine what types of packages they need. If such corporations bring packages that have high net social costs, part of the blame would seem to lie with the developing countries for not having conducted proper cost-benefit analyses in the first place.

Balance of Payments

We have pointed out the negative balance-of-payments effects sometimes associated with the restrictive business practices of transnationals. However, evidence suggests that some transnationals do bring about positive balance-of-payments effects in developing countries. A study covering over 100 firms in Colombia, India, Iran, Jamaica, Kenya, and Malaysia found that in some of the cases the balance-of-payments impact of transnational corporations was on the positive side—for example, 3 out of 11 in Jamaica,

5 out of 8 in Kenya, and 9 out of 53 in India.[36] However, it is true that the direct balance-of-payments effects on the whole were negative.[37] This position contrasts with another finding that concluded that "when all the direct effects on the balance-of-payments accounts are taken into consideration, the net result in developing countries is usually positive, though it is more visible in the case of extractive industries than of manufacturing."[38] We feel that this statement may be premature in view of the need for more thorough research. Even so, if restrictive business practices do prevail in these sectors, it could be argued that the net contribution to balance of payments is likely to be greater for individual developing countries than if they were not in existence.

Economic Growth

Theoretically, it is evident that injections of capital and technology are necessary for stimulating economic growth. Growth is vital for developing countries, given the low prevailing levels of real gross national output in such countries. By augmenting national output, transnationals can be said to be important agents of economic change. It is sometimes argued that the difference between gross domestic product and gross national product may be great because of foreign ownership of economic resources. There are also positive spread effects of transnational corporations, which can be growth-inducing as well—for example, training in certain rudimentary skills, demonstration effects in terms of new techniques, and the like. We have seen the role of transnational corporations in the export growth of manufactured goods of a large number of developing countries. Given the role of the manufacturing sector in overall economic activity, it is probably easy to imagine the importance of transnational corporations to growth. However, the growth-inducing effects are likely to be greater in the absence of restrictive output policies.

Economic Transformation

A related question is economic transformation. Transnationals can be important agents here in the sense that they bring new industries, new techniques, and the like that may create structural changes in particular developing countries. Such changes are vital for development. However, the overall effect of these changes might be greater in developing countries if the restrictive business practices that stifle structural changes were somehow brought under control.

Stimulus to Competition

Earlier we saw that restrictive business practices may prove harmful for competition. However, it could be argued that dominance of local markets by foreign firms may provide an inducement for stimulating local producers into a keener sense of competition, at least in the short term. In this sense, transnational firms can be said to be performing a positive, indirect competitive role by acting as a catalyst that stimulates competitive responses on the part of local firms. We do not know to what extent this argument holds in developing countries. Evidence from developed countries does, however, suggest that "foreign rivalry" can at times provide doses of competitive effervescence. The American challenge and industrial response in France during the late 1960s and early 1970s illustrate this point. In this light, it should be remembered that firms in developing countries are often small and competitively weak against larger foreign firms, so that in the long run this argument may fail to be a very convincing one. At any rate, it can be argued that the positive effects on competition are likely to be greater in the absence of such restrictive practices aimed at eliminating local firms.

Changes in Tastes and Demand

Changes in tastes and demand can be a positive aspect for macroeconomic activity since they can add to greater employment, greater consumer satisfaction, and greater injection of capital and technology. Transnational corporations are constantly in search of new markets, new means of consumer satisfaction, and the like. Thus, it may be said that their role in economic activity in developing countries, especially those engaged in the internal markets of such countries—namely, import-substituting type of activities—may be greater than is sometimes allowed for. However, this is sometimes interpreted as a cost, since such corporations, it could be argued, do not cater to social needs as such but to the demand of particular income groups (more affluent groups), thereby aggravating social contradictions in developing countries. Even here, restrictive business practices tend to limit employment creation and technological diffusion, for example. Thus, the potential benefits here would seem to be greater if one assumed the nonexistence of such practices.

CONCLUSION

On balance, the evidence seems to suggest that in spite of some benefits that can be attributed to transnational corporations, the potential contribution of such corporations to development in the Third World would tend to be much greater if such restrictive practices were effectively controlled. This is so because such practices tend to exert a negative influence on the development process in many Third World countries. These practices in turn tend to circumscribe the benefits that can be associated with the operation of transnational corporations in developing countries. If, then, one is thinking of maximizing the net positive impact of transnationals in the Third World, regulation of restrictive business practices that operate as special constraints to Third World development would seem to be necessary. Through forms of control, the adverse effects of such practices conceivably could be kept to a minimum, and social welfare in many developing countries correspondingly could be increased under appropriate distributional assumptions. In Chapter 3, problems affecting the control of such practices in developing countries were examined.

7 POLICY ASPECTS OF RESTRICTIVE BUSINESS PRACTICES

So far, we have looked at restrictive business practices within the context of the competitive process of international firms. This study would be incomplete without some reference to the ongoing work on the international aspects of controlling the restrictive business practices of transnationals. Indeed, it would be surprising, given the nature of the problem so far discussed, if such attempts were nonexistent.

HISTORICAL ASPECTS

One of the earlier attempts at discussing restrictive business practices in the international context dates back to the Havana Charter, to which reference was made earlier. The objective of the charter, promulgated by the UN Conference on Trade and Employment, was to prevent private or public enterprises from engaging in restrictive business practices "whenever such practices have harmful effects on the expansion of production or trade."[1] However, the Havana Charter was specifically concerned with neither transnationals nor the impact of restrictive business practices as they relate to development. Its concern was universal.

124 CHAPTER 7

In 1952, a second treaty attempt in the area of restrictive business practices appeared in the form of the Draft Articles of Agreement proposed by the Ad Hoc Committee on Restrictive Business Practices of the Economic and Social Council (ECOSOC) of the United Nations.[2] The idea behind the treaty was that "members of the United Nations take appropriate measures and cooperate with one another with a view to achieving the objectives laid down in Article 46, paragraph 1 of Chapter 5 of the Havana Charter"[3]—namely, restrictive business practices found harmful to international trade. In this light, it was proposed that a permanent secretariat be established to deal with restrictive business practices complaints. However, not much came out of ECOSOC's efforts. One commentator described the achievements as "nothing more than history."[4] Parallel attempts by the Council of Europe in the area of restrictive business practices also failed to achieve much. One reason for this is that the council's work was largely intended to complement the work of ECOSOC. Thus, it expressed the conviction "that the draft agreement drawn up by the Ad Hoc Committee seemed to represent those minimum standards of any agreement in this field, to which a large number of countries could agree."[5]

Another attempt was that of the General Agreement on Tariffs and Trade (GATT), also in the 1950s. The idea was that GATT could afford the opportunity of examining the possibility of inserting provisions relating to restrictive business practices in international trade.[6]

UNCTAD AND RESTRICTIVE BUSINESS PRACTICES

Strictly speaking, however, the history of restrictive business practices of transnationals and their relationship to developing countries is of relatively recent origin. The attempts date only to this decade and began with the work of UNCTAD, which was formed in the 1960s. UNCTAD's existence seemed to be related to the need of developing countries to articulate their special interests at the level of international organization. Thus the organization has come to be known as a Third World forum. Indeed most of the international trade problems affecting such countries are reflected in UNCTAD's work.[7] Concern by UNCTAD in the area of restrictive business practices could be divided as follows: manufactures and semimanufactures, and technology. In relation to the first—manufactures and semimanufactures—Conference Resolution 73 of 1972 decided to establish the Ad Hoc Group of Experts on Restrictive Business Practices.[8] Another ad hoc group of experts was set up in 1974, and at the time of writing yet another ad hoc group had come into being. The basic aim of UNCTAD's ad hoc groups has been to shed greater light on restrictive business practices that are likely to adversely affect the trade and development of developing countries and to devise policy measures for these. For example, UNCTAD's Committee of Manufactures defined the objectives of the first ad hoc group as follows:

Identifying those practices that are likely to result in the acquisition and abuse of market power at the national and international levels;
Examining ways of improving the exchange of information on restrictive business practices between governments of developed and developing countries;
Examining the elements in the formulation of a model law or laws for developing countries on restrictive business practices;
Examining the possibility of formulating multilaterally acceptable principles on restrictive business practices that aim at remedying those practices likely to adversely affect the trade and development of developing countries.[9]

Some of the practices identified by UNCTAD's Ad Hoc Group of Experts have already been mentioned. In connection with the ways of improving the exchange of information on restrictive business practices, work has centered largely on the exchange of information between governments of developed and developing countries. In the report of the second ad hoc group, for example, the information is divided into the following two categories: (1) information already made public, and (2) information not made public or made public only partly.[10]

In this light, suggestions concerning consultation procedures have been made. Broad possibilities that have been suggested include the following:

Where a developing country believes that its trade and development interests are being adversely affected by restrictive business practices engaged in by a firm or firms in a developed country or countries, the developing countries should directly enter into consultations with that country or countries.
Where as a result of such consultations, it is agreed that a particular restrictive business practice or practices adversely affects, or is likely to adversely affect, the trade and development of the developing country in question, the countries in question should take appropriate measures to bring about agreed remedial action.
Where a satisfactory conclusion is reached as a result of the consultations, the countries concerned should notify the secretary general of UNCTAD of the nature of the restrictive business practices in question and the remedial action taken, in a form considered appropriate

by the countries concerned. If the countries so agree, the secretary general would propose a report for circulation to the states members in order that they may benefit from consultations.

Where a developed country undertakes an investigation or initiates legal proceedings, the results of which are likely to involve or to affect the trade and development interests of a developing country or countries, it should notify the latter as early as possible of such investigations or proceedings with a view to holding consultations on a bilateral basis so as to ensure that their views are taken into account.

To the extent that difficulties arise as between developing countries, similar consultation procedures should be followed.[11]

In 1976, the second ad hoc group of experts began discussions on the formulation of multilaterally acceptable principles and rules for the control of restrictive business practices.[12] The work was continued by the third ad hoc group of experts.[13] The following principles have been agreed upon:

Appropriate action should be taken in a mutually reinforcing manner at the national, regional, and international levels to eliminate restrictive business practices including those of transnational corporations adversely affecting international trade, particularly that of developing countries.

Collaboration between governments at bilateral and multilateral levels should be established, and where such collaboration has been established, it should be improved to facilitate the control of restrictive business practices.

Appropriate mechanisms should be devised at the international level to facilitate exchange and dissemination of information among governments.[14]

At the national and regional levels, the following areas of action have been recommended:

Improvement and effective enforcement of appropriate legislation for controlling restrictive business practices;

Elimination or control at the level of economic integration arrangements of all restrictive business practices impeding the free flow of goods in their intratrade;

Mechanisms at regional and subregional levels for dealing with information and the application of national laws and policies;

Elaboration of a model law to assist developing countries in developing appropriate legislation.[15]

Work is ongoing on the model law, and as yet no clear consensus exists as to what it should entail. At the time of writing, however, agreement was reached as to a voluntary set of principles for regulating restrictive business practices.

In the second area of restrictive business practices—namely, technology—major work has been concerned with drafting an international code of conduct. From the point of view of developing countries, one of the principles upon which the code should be based is "the elimination of restrictive business practices arising out of or affecting technology transactions."[16] Among the practices that such countries are keen to eliminate are the following:

Restrictions after expiration of arrangement;
Payments and other obligations after expiration of industrial property rights;
Grant-back provisions;
Limitations upon use of technology already imported;
Restrictions on adaptations;
Restrictions on research and sales, representations, or manufacturing arrangements related to competing or complementary technologies or products;
Tying arrangements;
Limitations on volume, scope of production, or field of activity;
Use of quality controls;
Restrictions in the use of personnel;
Price fixing;
Exclusive sales or representation agreements;
Export restrictions;
Obligations to use trademarks;
Restrictions on publicity;
Requirement to provide equity or to participate in management;
Unlimited or unduly long duration of arrangements;
Cartels/patent pools or cross-licensing arrangements.

Developed countries within UNCTAD also agreed in principle to eliminate some clauses in restrictive business practices, especially those relating to pricing, tying and limitation arrangements, and collusive behavior. There is, however, incomplete agreement with developing countries as to the range of practices to be eliminated. For example, according to the report of the Intergovernmental Group of Experts on an International Code of Conduct on Transfer of Technology on its sixth session, developed countries had agreed upon the elimination of fourteen clauses, whereas developing countries had agreed to the elimination of a much larger number. Also, it is not quite clear if the code should take a legal character or an essentially voluntary one. Developing countries seem to favor the former, while developed ones favor the latter.

Some brief comments are in order in terms of UNCTAD's work. Note that only the manufacturing sector and technology are explicitly covered by UNCTAD's work on restrictive business practices. We have seen the importance of restrictive business practices to the service sector, as well as to primary-sector activity. If one optimistically assumes that agreement is reached on the measures to be implemented by UNCTAD, it would appear that this is likely to have only a limited effect on the resolution of the problem, given the organization's present orientation. For this reason, UNCTAD could very well give a more complete representation of the issues by tackling the two presently ignored domains of restrictive business practices. Note, for example, that the Commodities Division of UNCTAD, which is concerned with primary-sector activity, does not directly concern itself with restrictive business practices. Second, the organization, although showing an interest in the role of transnational corporations in restrictive business practices in several of the studies cited, does not appear to approach aspects of controlling the activities of such corporations in a direct manner. For instance, the principles and rules concerning restrictive business practices, the identification of practices, and the model law not only relate to transnationals but to other enterprises as well. Likewise, restrictions on technology transfer are not confined to transnationals, though it is true they are the most important vehicles for transferring such technology. Public enterprises and state enterprises in developed countries are also active agents in transferring technology to developing countries. Further, technology-transfer arrangements take place, though to a still lesser extent, between developing countries. Some important exporters of technology in developing countries include Mexico, Brazil, Venezuela, Nigeria, India, Jamaica, and Egypt. Such countries will likely continue to play an increasing role in the international trade of technology as their comparative advantages increase with learning-by-doing-economies, among other things, and as strategies for collective self-reliance among developing countries take firmer shape. The idea behind collective self-reliance is to increase, through joint and concerted action, the contribution of developing countries to world trade and production.

Seen then in this light, regulatory action within UNCTAD does not exclusively concern transnational corporations. This aspect certainly introduces wider dimensions to the problem. UNCTAD has introduced the concept of preferential treatment for enterprises in developing countries. This differentiation could, however, go some way in facilitating desirable action against transnationals in the area of restrictive business practices.

OTHER CASES

Meanwhile, specific work on the regulation aspects of transnationals in the area of restrictive business practices is to be found in the following organizations: The OECD, the ILO, and the UN Centre on Transnational Corporations.

In 1976 the OECD, in a publication entitled *International Investment and Multinational Enterprises,* called on transnationals to

1. Refrain from actions which adversely affect competition in the relevant market by abusing a dominant position of market power by means of:
   —Anti competitive acquisitions
   —Predatory behaviour towards competition
   —Unreasonable refusal to deal
   —Anti competitive abuse of industrial property rights
   —Discriminatory pricing and using such pricing transactions between affiliated enterprises as a means of adversely affecting competition between enterprises.
2. Allow purchasers, distributors and licensees freedom to resell, export, purchase and develop their operations consistent with law, trade conditions, the need for specialization and sound commercial practice.
3. Refrain from participating in or otherwise purposely strengthening agreements which adversely affect or eliminate competition and which are not generally or specifically accepted under national or international legislation.
4. Be ready to consult and co-ordinate including the provision of information with competent authorities of countries whose interests are adversely affected.[17]

The guidelines also relate to such issues of technology as the following:

Transnationals should endeavour that their policies fit into scientific and technological policies and plans of the countries in which they operate and contribute to the development of national scientific and technological capacities including the establishment and improvement in host countries of their capacities to innovate.
The adoption of practices which permit the rapid diffusion of technology with due regard to the protection of industrial and intellectual property rights.
When granting licences for the use of industrial property rights, or when otherwise transferring technology, to do so on reasonable terms and conditions.[18]

In spite of this attempt, it is sometimes argued that the OECD guidelines lack much force simply because they do not have a legally binding character. Member states and enterprises are free to accept or reject them. We already saw the need for an appropriate legal framework for dealing with restrictive business practices of transnationals, especially when these relate to developing countries.

The ILO, while dealing with transnationals, deals essentially with the employment aspects of restrictive business practices. The subject of employment is broadly within the competence of that organization.[19] Thus, of direct relevance to the question of restrictive business practices in these terms is the recommendation that the opportunity should be given for the "promotion and advancement of nationals of host countries at all levels."[20] The position is sometimes taken that transnationals restrict employment possibilities for nationals in developing countries, especially in such key positions as management, marketing, engineering, research and development, and finance[21]—hence, its relevance to restrictive business practices.

Another point in the ILO's *Declaration of Principles* relates to the "conclusion of contracts with national enterprises for the manufacture of parts and equipment, to the use of local raw materials, and to the progressive promotion of the local processing of raw materials."[22] As we saw, restrictive business practices often tie import sources for the use of equipment and intermediate products as well as raw materials.

The ILO's *Declaration of Principles* is equally voluntary and suffers from the same criticism of voluntary guidelines for controlling the activities of transnationals. It is possible to argue, however, that these principles can perhaps play a role in influencing legal decisions on the matter and in creating a necessary public international climate for new corporate norms that may increase social and economic responsibility on the part of transnationals. This is best left to the test of time. Experience has proven, however, that big business is likely to respond most quickly to such social objectives when some recourse to the law is possible. Even so, remember that these approaches are not ultimate ones. In this sense, they could be regarded as useful initial approaches. We will then have to await the course of future action.

The most recent work in the United Nations pertaining to transnationals and restrictive business practices concerns the work of the UN Centre on Transnational Corporations. An intergovernmental working group established by this commission began work on a draft code on transnationals in 1974. This body was charged with "the formulation of the most comprehensive code of conduct relating to the activities of transnational corporations."[23] Given the disparate attempts at the international level, this may be considered as a useful "gap-bridging" effort. The program of work of the UN commission is "to secure international arrangements that promote the positive contribution of transnational corporations to national development goals and world economic growth while controlling and eliminating their negative effects."[24]

A preliminary code by the UN Centre on Transnational Corporations has been completed. Some of the main issues relating to restrictive business practices covered in the code are as follows:

Transnationals are required to respect the economic goals and development objectives of their host country; the general obligation of developed countries is to take necessary action to ensure that the activities of such corporations meet the above objectives.

Transnationals are required to contribute to the expansion of exports, particularly by avoiding the imposition of undue restrictions on exports by affiliates and by utilizing raw materials and other domestic resources in the developing countries. The same applies to excessive profits remittance, royalties, and fees.

Transfer pricing by transnationals should be controlled. In their intracorporate transactions transnationals should desist from the application of pricing principles that, in violation of the laws, regulations, and practices of the countries concerned, evade taxation or substantially reduce the tax base on which they are assessed or have adverse effects on competition, employment, technological development, credit policies, and balance-of-payments objectives. Arms-length-pricing principles are suggested as a substitute. Transnationals are further urged to disclose the principles applied in transfer pricing and all relevant information upon request by governmental authorities.

The code also introduces an element of unfair competition relating to consumer protection, found wanting in most international attempts aimed at controlling restrictive business practices. Transnationals are required, in accordance with national laws, regulations, and administrative practices of the countries concerned, to perform their operations in a manner not injurious to the health and safety of consumers. In particular, by means of labeling and advertising, transnationals should disclose to the public in the countries in which they operate all appropriate information of the contents of the products they produce or market in the countries concerned.[25]

The code, however, lacks the specific details of UNCTAD's, for example, and this probably shows the lead that UNCTAD has over it insofar as action-oriented proposals go. But it must be remembered that the UN Centre on Transnationals has only just begun to address itself to the problem, and, as mentioned earlier, its code is still of a preliminary nature.[26] It is also not quite clear what the final code will look like. For instance, should it be legally binding or voluntary, or should it represent a combination of both voluntary and legally binding features?

At the regional and subregional levels, mention was made in Chapter 4 on the work of the Caribbean Community, the Andean Pact, and Latin America in general. Indications are that similar attempts at controlling restrictive business practices are afoot in regional integration schemes in Africa, which are at the moment functioning far from adequately. However, work seems not to have gone very far beyond this, and action at the national level in developing countries seems to lack the momentum of the international. Yet, it is clear that considerable scope for action exists in developing countries for controlling the restrictive business practices of transnationals. It remains true, however, that this is likely to be influenced somewhat by the international climate.

Also, we are yet to see action by developed countries in controlling the external activities of their transnationals. Arguably, this, too, is contingent upon an international consensus. Country A may not want to move to impair the profit and growth motives of its transnationals unless corresponding action is taken by other parent countries of transnationals. Corporate business people constitute a powerful lobby in industrialized countries, and this fact remains whether or not joint action is taken by developed countries to control their overseas activities. The point is, however, that business and governmental resistance may both be greater if action is taken by Country A while Countries B–Z do not follow suit. Moral force for action will tend to be greater if action based on consensus is taken.

Meanwhile, a special dilemma seems to face developing countries. Most of these countries depend on transnationals in one way or the other to stimulate their development efforts. If harmonious legal measures are lacking on the part of these countries, it could be argued that transnationals may play off one country at the expense of others—an experience common to economic integration schemes in many developing countries. This argument indicates why a common policy seems necessary. Laws in themselves do not seem to be enough. Equally important are national policies toward foreign firms, including incentives, infrastructural considerations, wage policy, attitude toward local firms, technology, and the like. In a sense, the question of preferential treatment is not only applicable to whether firms in developing countries are exempted from restrictive business practices laws and the extent of this exemption; given the different levels of development among developing countries themselves, allowance may also have to be made for this consideration in terms of the common policy referred to earlier.

To sum up, in terms of international negotiations on the matter and the issues at hand, the record is as yet far from impressive. We have seen the proliferation of codes, a growing awareness of the problem, but little policy action.

Meanwhile, proposals for establishing a New International Economic Order call for an increasing transfer of real resources from developed to developing countries. If one assumes that transnationals (given their existing role in the economic activity of developing countries) are to be an important consideration in the process of accelerated resource transfer to such countries, one must also concede the possibility of an increased proliferation of restrictive business practices. It follows that developing countries are unlikely to benefit to the fullest extent possible in the proposed world economic structure unless such practices are brought under regulatory control. The same goes for the Lima target of accelerated industrial development in developing countries by the year 2000. By then it is hoped that the present developing countries' share in world industrial output, estimated currently at around 8 percent, will have increased to 25 percent.

However, evidence points to increased protectionism by developed countries at this juncture of international economic relations. The downturn of world economic activity is often cited as an important consideration determining this state of affairs. One implication of this situation may well be the relaxation of domestic control measures in parent countries of transnationals, much to the detriment of developing countries. This remains so in spite of the limitations of such measures. It can also mean limited interest on the part of developed countries to control restrictive business practices at the international level for fear that this may jeopardize the international business climate for transnationals. Historically, for example, such practices, as evidenced by cartel activities, tend to be quite prevalent during periods of economic downturn.

CONCLUSIONS

This study was essentially an exploratory survey aimed at locating the restrictive business practices of transnational corporations in a wider framework of analysis of development. Concepts of gross market imperfection, such as those relating to oligopoly behavior as well as dynamic features of competition were used and modified accordingly to fit the purpose of our analysis.

In particular, we found considerations relating to the legal environment under which transnational firms operate to be of relevance. This was so because legal controls over the restrictive business practices aspects of transnational corporations as they affect developing countries were found to be usually either nonexistent or inadequate. Negative effects of restrictive business practices of transnational corporations were found to be possible in most key areas of development—for example, employment creation, technology, rural development, natural resource development, levels of real output, savings and investment, income distribution, aspects of resource misallocation, aspects of social welfare, and problems of economic dependency in terms of imports and exports. On the positive side of the equation, and at a general level, transnational corporations were found to be important potential sources of growth and transformation in developing countries, but the overall contribution of such corporations to development in the Third World seemed to be far from optimal because of the existence of restrictive business practices that limit the contribution such corporations could potentially make to development.

From our analysis, it would seem that most of the criticisms found in the literature against the operations of transnational corporations in developing countries are strongly associated with the use of restrictive business practices.

The problem of inadequate data has been repeatedly evident throughout this study. While this lack would seem to operate as an obstacle to in-depth analyses of the problem of restrictive business practices and development, the available data do seem to provide a sufficient basis for a general and exploratory treatment of the subject matter, such as the one we have attempted here. However, more rigorous empirical research can shed greater light on the importance of restrictive business practices to development and can, in particular, facilitate the analysis of such effects. It is hoped that our research may stimulate efforts in that direction—in particular, quantification of the real developmental impact.

In this context, future lines of research could be concentrated on particular industries in developing countries—for example, sugar, mining, or some key manufacturing sectors (including those using highly modern technology and those not very technology-intensive). From here, it might be possible to look at the matter in sectoral terms so that comparative sectoral analyses could be conducted. It might then also be possible to compare country experience. Another approach could entail the study of particular practices only—say, transfer pricing, the element of price collusion, territorial market allocation arrangements, boycotts, and the use of political considerations to strengthen market power.

Regardless of what direction future research takes, attempts to regulate the activities of transnationals—in particular, restrictive business practices aspects as they affect the Third World—are clearly a key consideration to any meaningful international development policy. Given the worldwide nature of such corporations, what seems equally clear is that bold action at both the national and international levels is necessary to minimize special disadvantages that accrue to developing economies as a result of the present legal and institutional framework governing the activities of transnationals in the area of restrictive business practices.

NOTES

INTRODUCTION

1. Some of these problems include relatively low per capita income, high rates of unemployment and underemployment, low levels of savings and capital formation, inadequate infrastructure, low real rates of economic growth, specialization in one or two primary products, an almost nonexistent industrial structure, a high incidence of absolute poverty, and the like. In a sense, these problems are not necessarily confined to countries located in Africa, the Caribbean, Latin America, and Asia. "Development" areas do exist in industrial societies, such as the United Kingdom, the United States, France, and Italy, though the problems posed here may represent less stark anomalies than those found in the contrast between the industrialized and developing worlds. But even in developing countries, "problems of development" are often problems as they affect lower socioeconomic groups. We must keep this point in mind throughout the study.

2. The subject of development studies, for example, is now taught in many leading European and North American universities, as well as in universities in developing countries. Several journals specializing in the subject are now on the academic market.

3. For the purpose of this study, transnational corporations are regarded as firms that have their production bases in one or more foreign countries. More often than not, these firms emanate from developed countries.

138 NOTES

CHAPTER 1

1. See OECD, *Market Power and the Law* (Paris, 1970), p. 13.
2. Definition adopted by United Nations Conference on Trade and Employment, *The Havana Charter, Final Act* (New York, 1948), p. 35.
3. See, for example, OECD, *Annual Reports on Competition Policy in OECD Member Countries* (Paris, various issues).
4. See OECD, *Glossary of Terms Relating to Restrictive Business Practices A-2* (Paris), pp. 12–13.
5. See P. Sraffa, "The Laws of Returns under Competitive Conditions," *Economic Journal* (December 1926).
6. J. Robinson, *The Economics of Imperfect Competition* (London: Macmillan, 1933).
7. E. H. Chamberlain, *The Theory of Monopolistic Competition* (Cambridge, Mass.: Harvard University Press, 1933).
8. An illustration of the firm in this state can be found in most elementary textbooks on economics, to which the interested reader is referred.
9. See OECD, *Market Power,* p. 50.
10. Sraffa, "Laws of Returns."
11. See, for example, Denis O'Brien, "Mergers—Time to Turn the Tide," *Lloyds Bank Review,* no. 130 (October 1978):32–44.
12. A. Cournot, *Researches in the Mathematical Principles of the Theory of Wealth* (1838), trans. N. T. Bavon (New York: Macmillan, 1972).
13. Allowance can be made for the fact that firms adjust output instead of prices to give some flexibility to the model.
14. Chamberlain, *Monopolistic Competition.*
15. These are not uncommon practices found in restrictive business practices complaints in the EEC, for example.
16. G. J. Stigler, "A Theory of Oligopoly," *Journal of Political Economy* (February 1964).
17. H. H. von Stackelberg, *The Theory of the Market Economy,* trans. A. Peacock (London: William Hodge & Company, 1952).
18. See C. J. Hawkins, *Theory of the Firm* (London: Macmillan, 1973), p. 32, for some treatment.
19. See A. Kaplan, J. Dirlam, and R. Lanzilloti, *Pricing in Big Business: A Case Approach* (Washington, D.C.: Brookings Institution, 1958); M. Colberg, D. Forbush, and R. Whittaker, *Business Economics—Principles and Cases,* 3rd. ed. (Homewood, Ill.: Richard D. Irwin, 1964); J. Markham, *Competition in the Rayon Industry* (Cambridge, Mass.: Harvard University Press, 1952); and C. Hession, "The Metal Container Industry," in W. Adams, ed., *The Structure of American Industry* (New York: Macmillan, 1961).
20. G. J. Stigler, "The Dominant Firm and the Inverted Umbrella," *Journal of Law and Economics* (October 1965).

21. J. Markham, "The Nature and Significance of Price Leadership," *American Economic Review* (December 1951).

22. R. Harrod, "Theory of Imperfect Competition Revised," in Harrod, ed., *Economic Essays* (London: Macmillan, 1952).

23. P. M. Sweezy, "Demand Conditions under Oligopoly," *Journal of Political Economy* (August 1939); and R. Hall and C. Hitch, "Price Theory and Business Behavior," *Oxford Economic Papers* (May 1939).

24. See, for example, G. J. Stigler, "The Kinky Oligopoly Demand Curve and Rigid Prices," *Journal of Political Economy* (October 1947); Markham, "Price Leadership"; and P. Pashigian, "Conscious Parallelism and the Kinky Oligopoly Demand Curve," *American Economic Review, Papers and Proceedings* (May 1967).

25. See Markham and Pashigian, ibid.

26. See, for example, H. Simon, "On the Concept of Organizational Goal," *Administrative Science Quarterly* (June 1964); Simon, "Theories of Decision Making in Economics and Behavioral Science," *American Economic Review* (1959); A. Papandreou, "Some Basic Problems in the Theory of the Firm," in B. Haley, ed., *A Survey of Contemporary Economics,* vol. 2 (Homewood, Ill.: Richard D. Irwin, 1952); O. Williamson, "Managerial Discretion and Business Behavior," *American Economic Review* (December 1963); Williamson, *The Economics of Discretionary Behavior* (Englewood Cliffs, N.J.: Prentice-Hall, 1964); and Williamson, *Corporate Control and Business Behavior* (Englewood Cliffs, N.J.: Prentice-Hall, 1970).

27. See, for example, E. Penrose, *The Growth of Firms, Middle East Oil and Other Essays* (London: Frank Cass, 1971).

28. Namely, transnational corporations in the mining sector.

29. See S. Aaronovitch and M. Sawyer, *Big Business* (London: Macmillan, 1975).

30. See J. Schumpeter, *The Theory of Economic Development* (Cambridge, Mass.: Harvard University Press, 1934); and Schumpeter, *Capitalism, Socialism and Democracy* (London: Unwin University Books, 1954).

31. Schumpeter, *Capitalism, Socialism and Democracy,* p. 83.

32. Ibid.

33. Ibid. p. 82.

34. See J. K. Galbraith, *American Capitalism* (London: Hamish Hamilton, 1957), p. 91.

35. See A. Hunter, "The Control of Monopoly," *Lloyds Bank Review* (October 1956).

36. See J. Jewkes, D. Sawers, and R. Stillerman, *The Sources of Invention* (London; Macmillan, 1958), p. 31. Although the study is not extended to the 1970s, the basic contention still holds.

37. Ibid., p. 90.

38. Ibid., p. 85.

39. See J. M. Clark, "Competition, Static Models and Dynamic Aspects," *American Economic Review* (May 1955); Clark, *Competition as a Dynamic Process*

(Washington, D.C.: Brookings Institution, 1961); J. Downie, *The Competitive Process* (London: Macmillan, 1958); and E. Kantzenbach, *Die Funktionsfahigkeit des Wettbewerbs* (Gottingen: Van Den Hoeck and Ruprecht, 1967).

40. A. Berle and G. Means, *The Modern Corporation and Private Property* (New York: Macmillan, 1932); J. S. Bain, *Barriers to New Competition* (Cambridge, Mass.: Harvard University Press, 1956); G. J. Stigler, ed., *Business Concentration and Price Policy* (Princeton, N.J.: Princeton University Press, 1955); and Galbraith, *American Capitalism.*

41. Galbraith, *American Capitalism.*

42. This has been confirmed in recent studies by the OECD on industrial concentration and restrictive business practices.

43. For some evidence, see S. J. Prais, *The Evolution of Giant Firms in Britain* (Cambridge: Cambridge University Press, 1976).

44. See OECD, *Mergers and Competition Policy* (Paris, 1974).

45. Ibid.
46. Ibid.
47. Ibid.
48. Ibid.
49. Ibid.
50. Ibid.
51. Ibid.
52. Ibid., p. 9; see also *Cartel Office Report* (Bonn: West German Government, 1971).
53. Ibid.
54. Ibid.
55. Ibid., p. 7.
56. Ibid.
57. Ibid. Of course, in terms of the overall economy, concentration ratios rose.
58. Ibid.
59. Ibid.
60. Ibid.
61. Ibid.

62. See Monopolies Commission, *Survey of Mergers 1958—68* (London: Department of Trade and Indusry, 1970); and *A Review of Monopolies and Mergers* (Cmnd. 7198).

63. Ibid.

64. See UNCTAD, *Review of Major Developments in the Area of Restrictive Business Practices,* TD/3/C.2/159 (1975), p. 7.

65. O'Brien, "Mergers."

66. OECD, *Mergers and Competition Policy.*

67. A. K. Young, "Internationalization of the Japanese General Trading Companies," *Columbia Journal of World Business* (Spring 1974).

68. See OECD, *Aggregate Rebate Cartels* (Paris, 1972); OECD, Committee of Experts on Restrictive Business Practices, *Export Cartels* (Paris, 1974); and OECD,

Annual Reports on Competition Policy in OECD Member Countries, no. 2 (1973) and no. 1 (1974).

69. See ibid., *Export Cartels* and OECD, *Mergers and Competition Policy.*

70. N. Kaldor, "Market Imperfections and Excess Capacity," *Economic Journal* (1935): 30-50.

71. J. K. Galbraith, "Monopoly and the Concentration of Economic Power," in H. Eilles, ed., *A Survey of Contemporary Economics* (Philadelphia, 1948), p. 107.

72. Schumpeter, *Capitalism, Socialism and Democracy.*

73. Ibid.

74. J. Kipling, "Why Mergers Miscarry," *Harvard Business Review* (1967).

75. S. R. Reid, *Mergers, Management and the Economy* (New York: McGraw-Hill, 1968).

76. A. Singh, *Takeovers* (Cambridge: Cambridge University Press, 1971).

77. G. Meek, *Disappointing Marriage: A Study of the Gains from Mergers* (London: Cambridge University Press, 1977).

78. G. Meek and G. Whittington, "Giant Companies in the United Kingdom 1948—1969," *Economic Journal* 85 (1975): 824-43.

79. J. F. Pickering, *Industrial Structure and Market Conduct* (London: Martin Robertson, 1974).

80. Jewkes, Sawers, and Stillerman, *Sources of Invention, p. 31.*

81. See Monopolies Commission, *A Review of Monopolies and Mergers.*

82. OECD, *Mergers and Competition Policy,* chap. 1.

83. See J. Gennard, *The Economic and Technological Environment* (London: Open University Press, 1976), p. 31.

84. See K. Cowling and D. Mueller, "The Social Costs of Monopoly Power," *Economic Journal* (December 1978): 727-48.

85. See OECD, *Market Power and the Law.*

86. Ibid.

87. Ibid.

CHAPTER 2

1. It is not customary to incorporate X-efficiency considerations into these types of analyses; however, they do seem relevant.

2. J. R. Hicks, *Capital and Growth* (Oxford: Oxford University Press, 1965).

3. See A. Smith, *An Inquiry into the Nature and Causes of the Wealth of Nations,* E. Cannan, ed. (New York: Modern Library, 1977).

4. See Hicks, *Capital and Growth.*

5. Ibid.

6. See N. Kaldor, "Capital Accumulation and Economic Growth," in D. Hague, ed., *The Theory of Capital* (London: Macmillan, 1961).

7. T. Malthus, *An Essay on Population* (London, 1924).

8. J. A. Schumpeter, *The Theory of Economic Development* (Cambridge, Mass.: Harvard University Press, 1934).

9. See W. A. Lewis, "Economic Development and Unlimited Supplies of Labour," *The Manchester School* (1954); and Lewis, *The Theory of Economic Growth* (New York: Homewood, 1955). See also R. Nurkse, "Excess Population and Capital Construction," *Malayan Economic Review* (October 1957).

10. See, for example, G. Ranis and H. Fei, "A Theory of Economic Development," *American Journal of Economics* (September 1961).

11. Reference has already been made to Kaldor's observation.

12. Lewis, "Economic Development."

13. See B. Higgins, *Economic Development* (New York: Norton, 1959); and R. Ekaus, "The Factor Proportions Problem in Underdeveloped Areas," *American Economic Review* (1955).

14. J. Boeke, *Economics and Economic Policy of Dual Societies* (Haarlem: H. D. Willink, 1953). This study was based largely on empirical work conducted in the Dutch East Indies.

15. R. Nurkse, *Problems of Capital Formation in Underdevelped Countries* (Oxford: Oxford University Press, 1953).

16. W. Rostow, *The Stages of Economic Growth* (Cambridge: Cambridge University Press, 1963).

17. Ibid., p. 5.

18. Ibid., p. 7.

19. Ibid., p. 8.

20. Ibid.

21. Ibid., p. 6.

22. Ibid., p. 9.

23. A Hirschman, *Strategy of Economic Development* (New Haven, Conn.: Yale University Press, 1958); and J. R. Hicks, *Value and Capital* (Oxford: Oxford University Press, 1963), p. 122.

24. P. Bauer and B. Yamey, *The Economics of Underdeveloped Countries* (London: Cambridge University Press, 1957).

25. See E. Hagen, *On the Theory of Social Change: How Economic Growth Begins* (London: Tavistock Publications, 1964); A. Gershenkron, *Economic Backwardness in Historical Perspective* (Cambridge, Mass.: Harvard University Press, 1968); and B. Hoselitz, "Noneconomic Factors in Economic Development," *American Economic Review* 47 (1957).

26. See M. Todaro, *Economics for a Developing World* (London: Longman, 1977).

27. G. Myrdal, *Economic Theory and Underdeveloped Regions* (London: Druckworth, 1959).

28. Ibid., p. 51.

29. C. Kindleberger, *The Terms of Trade: A European Case Study* (New York: Wiley, 1956).

30. A. Cairncross, "World Trade in Manufactures since 1900," *Economia Internazionale* (November 1955).

31. See R. Baldwin, *Economic Development and Growth* (New York: John Wiley, 1966).

32. Policymakers of many newly politically independent countries began to stress the need to industrialize. Import substitution policies in Latin America, however, had a much earlier history, but the forces at work were the same.

33. Recent development plans, for example, give testimony to this.

34. See UNCTAD, *A Comprehensive Strategy for Expanding and Diversifying the Export Trade of the Developing Countries in Manufactures and Semimanufactures,* TD/185 (1975).

35. See F. Benham, *Economic Aid to Underdeveloped Countries* (London: Oxford University Press, 1961); and P. Bauer, *United States and Indian Economic Development* (Washington, D.C.: American Enterprise Association, 1959).

36. See J. Behrman, "Promoting Development through Private Direct Investment," *American Economic Review, Papers and Proceedings* (May 1960); W. A. Lewis, "The Industrialization in the British West Indies," *Caribbean Economic Review* (May 1950); and Caribbean Commission, *Industrial Development in the Caribbean* (Port of Spain, 1952).

37. See A. Frank, *Capitalism and Underdevelopment in Latin America* (London: New Left Review, 1968); O. Sunkel and P. Paz, *El sub desarrollo Latino-Americo y la teoria del desarrollo* (Mexico: Siglo Veintiuno, 1970); O. Sunkel, "Big Business and Dependencia," *Foreign Affairs* 50, no. 3 (1972); N. Girvan, *Foreign Capital and Economic Underdevelopment in Jamaica* (Jamaica: University of the West Indies, 1971); and C. Furtado, *Los Estados Unidos y el sub desarrollo a America Latino* (Lima: Instituto de Estudios Peruanos, 1971).

38. See N. Girvan, *Multinational Corporations and Dependent Underdevelopment in Mineral Export Economies,* Discussion Paper No. 87 (Yale University, 1970); and J. O'Connor, "International Corporations and Economic Underdevelopment," *Science and Society* 34 (1970).

39. Some of these conclusions were, however, not quite specific to the dependency school and were the findings of independent analysts. See, for example, P. Streeten and S. Lall, *Main Findings of a Study of Private Foreign Investment in Selected Developing Countries,* UNCTAD, TD/B/C.3/111 (1973); and UNCTAD, *Transfer of Technology,* TD/106 (1971).

40. M. Wionczek, in R. Vernon, ed., *Latin America Views the Foreign Investor* (New York: Praeger, 1965).

41. Import substitution industrialization in Latin America and the Caribbean is often cited in support of this.

42. In other words, to make economic peripheries less center-oriented.

43. See Frank, *Capitalism and Underdevelopment;* and S. Amin, *L'accumulation à l'echelle mondiale. Critique de la theorie du sous development* (Paris: Anthropos, 1971).

44. See P. Baran and P. Sweezy, *The Political Economy of Growth* (New York: Monthly Review Press, 1968).

45. Ibid.

46. W. Lenin, *Imperialism, the Highest Stage of Capitalism* (Hamburg, 1921); and J. Hobson, *The Export of Capital* (London: Constable, 1914).
47. Reference, for example, was made of this.
48. Transnational corporations have attracted attention only during the past two decades or so. It should be noted that traditional theory of the firm does not generally extend to an analysis of transnational corporations.
49. See F. Long, "Restrictive Business Practices, Multinational Corporations and Problems of Rural Development," *CERES,* FAO vol. 67 (1979).
50. UN, *Multinational Corporations in World Development* (New York, 1973).
51. Ibid., p. vi.
52. See, for example, report by the UNCTAD Secretariat, *Restrictive Business Practices* (Santiago, 1972), as well as subsequent reports by ad hoc groups of experts. The major concern is for a model law on restrictive business practices and the formulation of multilaterally acceptable principles and rules for the control of such practices.
53. UN General Assembly resolutions 3201 (S–VI) and 3202 (S–VI) of May 1974.
54. Ibid.
55. Ibid.
56. One of the oldest schools in development is the Institute of Social Studies in Holland. This antieconomism has been an important feature of that school. Likewise, the Institute of Development Studies, Sussex, one of the first Anglo-Saxon institutions in "development studies," has consistently criticized this approach to development.
57. See Todaro, *Economics for a Developing World.*
58. Ibid., p. 87.
59. D. Seers and R. Jolly, "The Brain Drain and the Development Process," in G. Ranis, ed., *The Gap between Rich and Poor* (London: Macmillan, 1972). In a more celebrated essay, "The Meaning of Development," Seers offers a more comprehensive critique to the traditional approach of development.
60. Ibid., p. 370.
61. See K. Griffin, *The Political Economy of Agrarian Change* (London: Macmillan, 1975).
62. See, for example, studies by the UN Research Institute on Social Development and recent studies by the ILO on rural poverty.
63. ILO, *Basic Needs: A One World Problem* (Geneva, 1976).
64. Ibid.

CHAPTER 3

1. See OECD, *Guide to Legislation on Restrictive Business Practices,* vols. 1, 2, 3, 4, 4th ed. (Paris, 1976), Section 1, p. 4.
2. Ibid.

3. Ibid.
4. See *Northern Pacific Company* v. *United States,* 356 U.S. 4 (1968).
5. OECD, *Guide to Legislation,* p. 5.
6. Ibid.
7. Ibid.
8. Ibid.
9. Ibid.
10. Ibid.
11. Ibid.
12. Ibid.
13. Ibid.
14. Ibid.
15. Ibid.
16. Ibid.
17. Ibid.
18. Ibid., Section United Kingdom, p. 3.
19. See, for example, Monopolies and Restrictive Business Practices Commission, *Report on Collective Discrimination* (London, 1955).
20. OECD, *Guide to Legislation,* Section United Kingdom.
21. See Section 1 of Restrictive Trade Practices Act.
22. OECD, *Guide to Legislation,* Section United Kingdom, p. 7.
23. Ibid., p. 4.
24. Ibid., p. 6.
25. See OECD, *Guide to Legislation,* Germany, Part 1, p. 1.
26. Ibid.
27. Ibid., p. 3.
28. Ibid., p. 4.
29. Ibid.
30. Ibid.
31. Ibid.
32. Ibid. See Section entitled "Action against Restraints of Competition of 1957" as amended.
33. Ibid., p. 11.
34. OECD, *Guide to Legislation,* Section 1, France, p. 3.
35. Ibid.
36. Ibid.
37. Ibid.
38. Ibid.
39. Ibid. Section General Provision, Article 62.
40. Contained in OECD, *Guide to Legislation.*
41. OECD, *Guide to Legislation,* Section Netherlands, Introduction to Section 1, p. 3.
42. Ibid.
43. Ibid.
44. Ibid.

45. OECD, *Guide to Legislation,* Section Japan, Introduction to Section 1, p. 2.

46. Ibid.

47. UNCTAD, *Informational Requirements for the Control of Restrictive Business Practices Originating with Firms of Developed Countries,* TD/B/C.2/156 (1975).

48. See EEC, *Official Journal of the European Community,* no. 13 (Brussels, February 1962).

49. See UNCTAD, *Control of Restrictive Business Practices in the European Economic Community* (New York, 1977), p. 9.

50. See EEC, *Official Journal.*

51. Ibid.

52. Ibid.

53. Ibid.

54. Ibid.

55. See F. Long, *The EEC and ACP—Science and Technology,* report to Commonwealth Secretariat (London, 1978).

56. See C. Greenhill, "UNCTAD: Control of Restrictive Business Practices," *Journal of World Trade Law* 67, no. 12 (1978).

57. Ibid.

58. For a discussion, see OECD, *Market Power and the Law,* in particular, Part 2.

59. See UNCTAD, *Review of Major Developments in the Area of Restrictive Business Practices,* TD/B/C.2/159 (1975).

60. See UNCTAD, *Restrictive Business Practices Issues for Consideration in the Context of Determining Elements of a Model Law or Laws on Restrictive Business Practices for Developing Countries,* TD/B/C.2/160 (1975); and UN, *Control of Restrictive Business Practices in Latin America* (New York, 1975).

61. Resolution 73 (iii) of the UN Conference on Trade and Development.

62. See UNCTAD, *Restrictive Business Practices Issues,* p. 1.

63. See Article 30 of the Treaty Establishing the Caribbean Community (Chaguaramas, 1973).

64. Ibid.

65. Impressions as a result of personal conversations with officials of the Secretariat in 1977.

66. See UNCTAD, *Laws and Regulations to Control Restrictive Business Practices,* TD/B/C.2/AC.5, Misc. 1 (1974).

67. Ibid.

68. *The Monopolies and Restrictive Trade Practices Control and Prevention Ordinance* (Delhi: Government of India, November 1970).

69. Ibid.

70. For example, preferential treatment is a standing feature of proposals to set up a new international economic order.

71. For example, within the framework of collective self-reliance, which is a central theme of most of UNCTAD's recent debates.

72. See Government of Malaysia, *Guidelines for the Regulation of Acquisition of Assets, Mergers and Takeovers* (February 1974).
73. See UN, *Control of Restrictive Business Practices in Latin America.*
74. Ibid.
75. Ibid.
76. Ibid.
77. See Decision No. 24 of the Commission of the Cartagena Agreement.
78. UNCTAD, *Control of Restrictive Business Practices.*
79. Ibid.
80. Ibid.
81. This is brought out in White's study and is based largely on the Latin American experience.
82. Based on White's findings.
83. For example, UNCTAD's work in restrictive business practices appears to be taking this turn.

CHAPTER 4

1. UN, *Multinational Corporations in World Development* (New York, 1973), p. 13.
2. Ibid.
3. Ibid., p. 7.
4. Ibid.
5. Data extracted from UN sources.
6. Especially in the area of macroeconomic analysis.
7. See J. M. Keynes, *The General Theory of Employment, Interest and Money* (London: Harcourt and Brace, 1936), p. 135.
8. R. Hall and C. Hitch, "Price Theory and Business Behavior, *Oxford Economic Papers* (May 1939).
9. A. Papandreou, "Some Basic Problems in the Theory of the Firm," in B. Haley, ed., *A Survey of Contemporary Economics,* vol. 2 (Homewood, Ill.: Richard D. Irwin, 1952); O. Williamson, "Managerial Discretion and Business Behavior," *American Economic Review* (December 1963); and T. Scitovsky, "A Note on Profit Maximization and Its Implications," *Review of Economic Studies* (1943), reprinted in American Economic Association, *Readings in Price Theory* (London: Allen & Unwin, 1953).
10. D. R. Roberts, *Executive Compensation* (Glencoe, Ill.: Free Press, 1959); J. W. McGuire et al., "Executive Incomes, Sales and Profits," *American Economic Review* (September 1962); and W. J. Baumol, "On the Theory of Oligopoly," *Economica* (1958).
11. E. Ames, *Economic Processes* (Homewood, Ill.: Richard D. Irwin, 1965); and M. J. Kafoglis, "Output of the Restrained Firm," *American Economic Review* (September 1969).

12. H. Averch and L. Johnson, "Behavior of the Firm under Regulatory Constraint," *American Economic Review* (December 1972).

13. This was one of the prime factors leading to overseas investments in the early part of this century.

14. See, for example, G. K. Helleiner, "Manufactured Exports from Less Developed Countries and Multinational Firms," *Economic Journal* (March 1973).

15. For example, import substitution within the context of extended regional market arrangements. The experience is well documented in Latin America and the Caribbean.

16. In this context, the case of Ireland as an underdeveloped country is relevant. See F. Long, "Foreign Direct Investment in an Underdeveloped European Economy—The Republic of Ireland," *World Development* 4 (1976).

17. See Y. Aharoni, *The Foreign Investment Decision Process* (Cambridge, Mass.: Harvard University Press, 1966).

18. R. Caves, "International Corporations: The Industrial Economics of Foreign Investment," *Economica* (February 1971).

19. For changing technological ascendancy, see R. Vernon, "International Investment and International Trade in the Product Cycle," *Quarterly Journal of Economics* 80 (1966); L. Wells, "Test of a Product Cycle Model of International Trade: U.S. Exports of Consumer Durables," *Quarterly Journal of Economics* 83 (1969); and S. Hirsch, *Location of Industry and International Competitiveness* (Oxford: Clarendon Press, 1967). For a discussion of the unique assets theory, see S. Hymer, "The Multinational Corporation and the Law of Uneven Development," in J. Bhagwati, ed., *Economics and World Order from the 1970s to 1990s* (London: Collier Macmillan, 1972).

20. In other words, aspects of unfair competition.

21. Vernon, "International Investment."

22. C. Vaitsos, *Intercountry Income Distribution and Transnational Enterprises* (Oxford: Oxford University Press, 1974).

23. See R. Vernon, *Storm over Multinationals* (London: Macmillan, 1977).

24. Ibid., p. 89

25. Ibid., p. 149.

26. E. Knickerbocker, *Oligopolistic Reaction and Multinational Enterprises* (Cambridge, Mass.: Harvard University Press, 1973).

27. See S. Hymer and B. Rowthorn, "Multinational Corporations and International Oligopoly: The American Challenge," in C. Kindleberger, ed., *The International Corporation* (Cambridge, Mass.: MIT Press, 1970); A. Singh, *Takeovers* (London: Cambridge University Press, 1971); and UNCTAD, *The Role of Transnational Corporations in the Trade in Manufactures and Semimanufactures of Developing Countries* (Geneva, 1975).

28. UNCTAD, ibid.

29. Ibid.

30. C. Edwards, "The Changing Dimension of Business Power," *St. John's Law Review* 44 (1970).

31. Caves, "International Corporations."

32. Ibid.
33. See, for example, N. Girvan, *Copper in Chile* (Mona: University of the West Indies, 1972).
34. See Vaitsos, *Intercountry Income Distribution,* p. 14.
35. S. Hymer and B. Rowthorn, *International Big Business 1957-67* (London: Cambridge University Press, 1971), p. 67.
36. See R. Vernon, *Restrictive Business Practices: The Operations of Multinational United States Enterprises in Developing Countries—Their Role in Trade and Development* (New York: UN, 1972), p. 16.
37. UN, *Multinational Corporations.*
38. Ibid., p. 6.
39. Ibid.
40. Ibid., p. 7.
41. See J. Behrman, *National Interests and Multinational Enterprises: Tensions among the North Atlantic Countries* (Englewood Cliffs, N.J.: Prentice-Hall, 1970); and R. Vernon, *Sovereignty at Bay: The Multinational Spread of United States Enterprises* (New York: Basic Books, 1971), p. 4.
42. UN, *Multinational Corporations,* p. 7.
43. See UNCTAD, *Role of Transnational Corporations* (1975).
44. UN, *Multinational Corporations,* p. 7.
45. A recent study by UNCTAD on transnational marketing groups brings this out.
46. UN, *Multinational Corporations.* This is particularly so in consumer durables and the capital goods sector.
47. R. Meller, *International Comparisons of Industrial Concentration in Latin America* (New York: National Bureau of Economic Research, n.d.).
48. R. Newfarmer and W. Mueller, *Multinational Corporations in Brazil and Mexico: Structural Sources of Economic and Noneconomic Power* (Washington, D.C.: U.S. Senate Subcommittee on Multinational Corporations, 1975).
49. J. Sourrouille, *The Impact of Transnational Corporations on Employment and Income: The Case of Argentina,* ILO Working Paper No. 7 (Geneva, 1976).
50. L. Willmore, "Direct Foreign Investment in Central American Manufacturing," *World Development* (1976): 499-518.
51. For example, agriculture and mining.
52. G. Beckford, *Persistent Poverty* (London: Oxford University Press, 1971).
53. These banks often followed "commercial business" opened up by transnational firms engaged in trade and production—for example, Lloyds Bank, Barclays, Royal Bank of Canada, First National City Bank, Chase Manhattan Bank, and so on.
54. For a country treatment, see F. Long, "Foreign Capital and Commercial Banking in Guyana," *Journal of World Trade* 2, no. 3 (May/June 1977).
55. See, for example, R. Newfarmer, *The International Market Power of Transnational Corporations: A Case Study of the Electrical Industry* (study prepared for the UNCTAD Secretariat, 1978).

56. See S. Lall, "Transnationals, Domestic Enterprises and Industrial Structure," *Oxford Economic Papers* 30 (July 1978): 227.

57. UN, *Multinational Corporations.*

58. Ibid., p. 18.

59. See "ACP and Mining," *Courier,* no. 49 (May/June 1978).

60. See, for example, H. Bruton, "The Import Substitution Strategy of Economic Development: A Survey," *Pakistan Development Review* (Summer 1970).

61. Ibid. Regional markets became important considerations as domestic markets reached their upper limit.

62. Ibid. Such a political climate is sometimes described as one of "investment by invitation," meaning, in a sense, a laissez faire attitude.

63. As, for example, in Latin America.

64. See Helleiner, "Manufactured Exports."

65. Ibid.

66. Ibid.

67. UN, *Multinational Corporations.*

68. For example, the British and American Virgin Islands, the Bahamas, and Bermuda.

69. Data obtained from UN, *Multinational Corporations.*

70. Ibid.

71. Ibid., Table 35.

72. Ibid.

73. The principle of political patronage comes to mind. A colony is naturally an extension of an imperial country. Firms from an imperial country investing in one of its colonies may receive preferential treatment over firms from competing imperial powers.

74. This has been particularly so in countries advocating a nonaligned foreign policy.

75. Based on a cursory examination of UN trade data from the 1960s onward.

76. See UNCTAD, *Role of Transnational Corporations* (1975), p. 2.

77. *Implications of Multinational Firms for World Trade and Investment and for U.S. Trade and Labor* (Washington, D.C.: U.S. Government Printing Office, 1973), p. 4.

78. See UN, *Multinational Corporations,* p. 15.

79. Ibid., p. 7.

80. *Implications of Multinational Firms,* p. 4.

81. Ibid.

82. UN, *Multinational Corporations,* p. 7.

83. M. Kirdon, *Western Capitalism since the War* (London, 1968), p. 4.

84. See UN, *Multinational Corporations,* p. 7; and John H. Dunning, "United Kingdom Transnational Enterprises in Manufacturing and Resource-Based Industries and Trade Flows of Developing Countries," study prepared for the UNCTAD Secretariat, n.d.

85. HWWA report, *Die Auslandstätigkeit der Deutschen Multinationalen Unternehmen,* no. 31 (Hamburg, 1975), p. 8.

86. HWWA estimates.

87. See, for example, S. Hirsch and Z. Adar, "Firm Size and Export Performance," *World Development* (July 1974): 41–47.

88. See UNCTAD, *The Role of Transnational Corporations in the Marketing and Distribution of Exports and Imports of Developing Countries,* TD/B/C.2/197 (1978).

89. Helleiner, "Manufactured Exports."

90. Ibid.

91. Ibid.

92. Ibid.

93. UNCTAD Briefing Paper No. 3 (December 1975), p. 2.

94. J. Katz, "Technology, Dynamic Comparative Advantage and Bargaining Power," in B. Cohen, ed., *Multinational Firms and Asian Exports* (New Haven, Conn.: Yale University Press, 1975), p. 10.

95. See F. Fajnzbler, *Sistema industrial y exportacion de manufactures: Analysis de la experiencia brasilers* (Chile: Economic Commission for Latin America, November 1970), p. 264.

96. *Implications of Multinational Firms,* p. 380.

97. Diaz Alejandro, "Colombian Imports and Import Controls in 1970/71: Some Quantifiable Features" (Yale University Economic Growth Center Paper No. 182, July 1973).

98. J. R. de la Torre, "Exports of Manufactured Goods from Developing Countries Marketing Factors and the Role of Foreign Enterprise" (Ph.D. thesis, Graduate School of Business Administration, Harvard University, 1970), p. 161.

99. See Reserve Bank of India, *Foreign Collaboration in Indian Industry* (Bombay, 1968).

100. *Implications of Multinational Firms,* pp. 378, 380.

101. See *Mexico's Manufactured Exports: Growth, Problems and Prospects,* IBRD/IDA Report No. 79-ME (Washington, D.C.: 1973), p. 2.

102. Board of Investments, *Annual Report* (Makati: Government of the Philippines, 1971).

103. See Cohen, *Multinational Firms,* p. 10.

104. Ibid.

105. See A. Hone, "Multinational Corporations and Multinational Buying Groups: Their Impact on the Growth of Asia's Exports of Manufactures—Myths and Realities," *World Development* (February 1974).

106. *Implications of Multinational Firms.*

107. HWWA report, *Die Auslandstätigkeit der Deutschen Multinationalen Unternehmen,* p. 54.

108. Ibid.

109. Ibid.

110. Hone, "Multinational Corporations."

111. These are based on provisional estimates by UNCTAD.

CHAPTER 5

1. See UNCTAD, *The Role of Transnational Corporations in the Trade in Manufactures and Semimanufactures of Developing Countries* (Geneva, 1975).
2. Ibid.
3. A defensive strategy may also prove harmful to competition, especially if the firm adopting the defensive strategy is a dominant type.
4. See UNCTAD, *Role of Transnational Corporations,* p. 6.
5. Ibid.
6. Ibid.
7. Ibid.
8. See UNCTAD, *Report of the Second Ad Hoc Group of Experts on Restrictive Business Practices,* TD/B/C.2.5/Rev. (1975), pp. 15-16.
9. R. Fine, "The Control of Restrictive Business Practices in International Trade: A Viable Proposal for an International Organization," *International Lawyer* 7, no. 3: 638.
10. See UNCTAD, *Report of the Intergovernmental Group of Experts on a Code of Conduct on Transfer of Technology,* TD/B/C.6/1 (1975).
11. See R. Vernon, *Restrictive Business Practices: The Operations of Multinational United States Enterprises in Developing Countries—Their Role in Trade and Development* (New York: 1972), p. 4.
12. G. Beckford, *Persistent Poverty* (London: Oxford University Press, 1971).
13. This has been widely documented in various studies on plantation agriculture.
14. Beckford, *Persistent Poverty.*
15. Ibid., p. 23.
16. Ibid., p. 27.
17. Ibid., p. 118.
18. See Eric Williams, *Capitalism and Slavery* (Chapel Hill: University of North Carolina Press, 1948).
19. Beckford, *Persistent Poverty.*
20. Ibid., p. 129.
21. See F. Long, "Corporate Plantations in the Guyanese Sugar Industry and Development," diss., Oxford University, 1975.
22. Beckford, *Persistent Poverty,* p. 130.
23. M. K. Kabunda, "Multinational Corporations and the Installation of Externally Oriented Economic Structures in Contemporary Africa: The Example of Unilever-Zaire Group," in C. Widstrand, ed., *Multinational Firms in Africa* (Uppsala: Scandinavian Institute of African Studies, 1975).
24. Ibid.
25. Ibid.
26. Ibid.
27. Ibid.
28. UNCTAD, *Marketing and Distribution System for Bananas* (Geneva, 1974).

29.   See *United States of America* v. *United Fruit Company: Final Judgment,* U.S. District Court for the Eastern District of Louisiana, Civil Action No. 4560 (February 1958, consent decree); and *United States of America* v. *United Fruit Company: Amended Complaint,* District of Louisiana, Civil Action No. 4560 (January 1956).

30.   Ibid.

31.   Ibid.

32.   Ibid. See also S. May and G. Plaza, *The United Fruit Company in Latin America Study No. 7* (National Planning Association, United States Business Performance Abroad Series, 1959).

33.   UNCTAD, *Marketing and Distribution for Cocoa* (Geneva, 1975), p. 88.

34.   E. Penrose, *The Growth of Firms, Middle East Oil and Other Essays* (London: Frank Cass, 1971).

35.   Ibid., p. 185.

36.   M. Tanzer, *The Political Economy of International Oil and the Underdeveloped Countries* (London: Temple Smith, 1970), p. 17.

37.   Vernon, *Restrictive Business Practices,* p. 4.

38.   Ibid., p. 5.

39.   Ibid., pp. 5-6.

40.   Ibid., p. 8.

41.   Ibid.

42.   This situation has been modified to some extent as a result of growing state control over nonrenewable natural resources.

43.   Vernon, *Restrictive Business Practices,* p. 9.

44.   Ibid.

45.   See Yip Hoong, *The Development of the Tin Mining Industry of Malaya* (Kuala Lumpur: University of Malaya Press, 1968), pp. 19-20.

46.   Ibid., p. 22.

47.   Ibid., p. 21.

48.   Ibid., p. 150.

49.   In the matter of General Foods Corporation, see FTC Docket No. 8198, 59 FTC 706 (1961).

50.   See UN, *Restrictive Business Practices* (New York, 1973), p. 51.

51.   See U.S., Congress, Senate, Subcommittee on Antitrust and Monopoly of the Judiciary, Prices of Quinine, Quinidine, Hearings, Parts 1 and 2, 89th and 90th Cong., 1966-67; and EEC press release, July 1961.

52.   Ibid.

53.   Vernon, *Restrictive Business Practices.*

54.   We also note that import substitution activities may later reveal themselves as export activities, at least in part.

55.   See E. Epstein and K. Mirow, *Impact on Developing Countries of Restrictive Business Practices of Transnational Corporations in the Electrical Equipment Industry: A Case Study of Brazil,* study prepared for the UNCTAD Secretariat, 1977, p. 1.

56.   Ibid.

57. Ibid.
58. Ibid.
59. Ibid.
60. See R. Newfarmer, *The International Market Power of Transnational Corporations: A Case Study of the Electrical Industry,* study prepared for the UNCTAD Secretariat, 1978.
61. Ibid., p. 84.
62. Ibid.
63. Ibid.
64. Ibid.
65. "Saudis Take Firm Action on Inflated Tenders," *Financial Times,* February 24, 1977.
66. Ibid.
67. OECD, *Collusive Tendering* (Paris, 1976), pp. 16–22.
68. See UN, *Restrictions on Exports in Foreign Collaboration Agreements in the Republic of the Philippines* (New York, 1972), pp. 17–18.
69. Ibid., p. 17.
70. See A. Espiritu, "A Filipino Looks at Multinational Corporations," *Law and Development* (1977).
71. S. Lall, "Transfer Pricing by Multinational Manufacturing Firms," *Oxford Bulletin of Economics and Statistics* (August 1973).
72. See UNCTAD, *Restrictive Business Practices* (Geneva, 1971), p. 21.
73. See C. Vaitsos, *Intercountry Income Distribution and Transnational Enterprises* (Oxford: Oxford University Press, 1974).
74. See UNCTAD, *Restrictive Business Practices.*
75. UNCTAD, *Dominant Positions of Market Power of Transnational Corporations: Use of Transfer Pricing Mechanism,* ST/MD/6/Rev. 1 (Geneva, 1977).
76. Ibid.
77. U.S., Congress, *Implications of Multinational Firms for World Trade and for U.S. Trade and Labor,* report to the Committee on Finance (Washington, D.C.: U.S. Government Printing Office, February 1973), p. 315.
78. See C. Vaitsos "Considerations on Technological Requirements in Developing Countries with Observations on Technology Licensing Agreements," paper prepared for UNIDO Symposium on Problems and Prospects of Industrial Licensing in Developing Countries, New York, 1972.
79. Ibid.
80. Ibid.
81. C. Salehkhou, "Commercialization of Technology in Developing Countries: Transfer of Pharmaceutical Technology in Iran," Ph.D. thesis, New School for Social Research, New York, 1974.
82. *Business Asia,* January 28, 1977, p. 27.
83. See K. Subrahmanian and P. Pillai Mohanan, "Implications of Technology Transfer in Export Led Growth Strategy," *Economic and Political Weekly,* October 30, 1976.

84. R. Morgenstern and R. Mueller, "Multinational Corporations and Balance of Payments Impacts in Developing Countries: An Econometric Analysis of Export Pricing Behaviour," *Kyklos* (April 1974). The survey covered 534 firms in ten countries.

85. UNCTAD, *Major Issues Arising from the Transfer of Technology to Developing Countries* (UN Publication Sales No. E.75.11.D.2).

86. M. Odle, *Commercialization of Technology in the Caribbean,* preliminary report, 1977.

87. See R. Green, "The Peripheral African Economy and MNC," in Widstrand, *Multinational Firms.*

88. See ILO, *Tripartite Declaration of Principles concerning Multinational Enterprises and Social Policy* (Geneva, 1977).

89. UNCTAD, *Restrictive Business Practices.*

90. See UNCTAD, *Role of Transnational Corporations.*

91. See F. Long, "Foreign Capital and Commercial Banking in Guyana," *Journal of World Trade 2,* no. 3 (May/June 1977).

92. A familiar echo of UNCTAD's Group of Experts on Restrictive Business Practices.

CHAPTER 6

1. See G. Myrdal's reflections on economic development contained in Myrdal, *Economic Theory and Underdeveloped Regions* (London: Druckworth, 1959).

2. See ILO, *Basic Needs Strategy* (Geneva, 1976).

3. The contention is that it is here that the greatest inequalities occur. Also, the bulk of the population in most developing countries live in rural areas.

4. See C. Thomas, "Diversification and the Burden of Sugar to Jamaica," *New World 5,* nos. 1 and 2 (1969). See also G. Beckford, *Persistent Poverty* (London: Oxford University Press, 1972).

5. UN General Assembly Resolutions 3201 (S-V1) and 3202 (S-V1) of May 1974.

6. See the studies by N. Girvan, *Copper in Chile* (Mona: University of West Indies, 1972).

7. ILO, *Tripartite Declaration of Principles concerning Multinational Enterprises and Social Policy* (Geneva, 1977).

8. This would seem to follow conventional monopoly theory.

9. See C. Vaitsos, *Intercountry Income Distribution and Transnational Enterprises* (Oxford: Oxford University Press, 1974).

10. Part of the Lome Agreement is for the processing of these materials.

11. S. Lall and P. Streeten, *Main Findings of a Study of Private Foreign Investment in Selected Developing Countries* (Geneva: UNCTAD, 1973).

12. J. Schumpeter, *Capitalism, Socialism and Democracy* (London: Unwin University Books, 1954).

13. This is an open question, however. The fact that local resources are used seems to offer precious little difference to the issue at stake here. It is true, however, that it might be easier to control such resources.

14. ILO Basic Needs Strategy strongly advocates this position, for example.

15. This is borne out in several of UNCTAD's publications in the area of technology.

16. See UNCTAD, "Strengthening the Technological Capacity of Developing Countries," Resolution 87 (IV), 1976.

17. UNCTAD, *Transfer of Technology* (Geneva, 1976).

18. UNCTAD's work on the Code of Conduct for Technology has this as a major concern.

19. For example, this would follow from the kinked-demand-curve type of hypothesis cited earlier.

20. For instance, if it is assumed that tacit agreement is taken to raise prices, then there is no problem here.

21. This is widespread in a number of Latin American countries. The idea is to have appropriate countervailing power.

22. However, that is by no means a sufficient condition for development.

23. UNCTAD, *The Role of Transnational Corporations in the Trade in Manufactures and Semimanufactures of Developing Countries* (Geneva, 1975).

24. UNCTAD, *Dominant Positions of Market Power of Transnational Corporations: Use of Transfer Pricing Mechanism,* ST/MD/6/Rev. 1 (Geneva, 1977).

25. Ibid.

26. Lall and Streeten, *Main Findings.*

27. Namely, the opening of markets of industrialized countries so that there could be easy access of developing countries' exports to such markets.

28. OECD, *Export Cartels* (Paris, 1974).

29. OECD, *Market Power and the Law* (Paris, 1970).

30. The Research Centre on the New International Economic Order in Oxford is presently conducting work in this area.

31. UNCTAD, for example.

32. UN, *Multinational Corporations in World Development* (New York, 1973), p. 52.

33. C. Vaitsos, *Employment and Foreign Direct Investments in Developing Countries: Some Notes and Figures, Junta del Acuerdo de Cartagena,* Document J/Aj/35/Rev. 1 (Lima, 1973).

34. Ibid.

35. UN, *Multinational Corporations,* p. 49.

36. Lall and Streeten, *Main Findings.*

37. Ibid.

38. UN, *Multinational Corporations,* p. 54.

CHAPTER 7

1. See UN Conference on Trade and Employment, *Final Acts and Related Documents* (New York, 1948).
2. See R. Fine, "The Control of Restrictive Business Practices in International Trade: A Viable Proposal for an International Organization," *International Lawyer* 7, no. 3:646.
3. Ibid.
4. Ibid.
5. Ibid., p. 649.
6. Ibid.
7. For example, trade expansion among developing countries, exports of manufactured goods to developed countries, commodity trade, and so on.
8. UNCTAD Conference Resolution 73 (III).
9. UNCTAD, Committee of Manufactures Resolution 9 (VII) 1975.
10. UNCTAD, *Report of the Second Ad Hoc Group of Experts on Restrictive Business Practices on Its First Session* (Geneva, November 1975), p. 18.
11. Ibid.
12. See S. Lall, "Price Competition in the International Pharmaceutical Industry," *Oxford Bulletin of Economics and Statistics* (February 1978).
13. See UNCTAD, *The Formulation of Equitable Principles and Rules at National and International Levels for the Control of Restrictive Business Practices Adversely Affecting International Trade and Particularly That of Developing Countries* (Geneva, January 1976).
14. See UNCTAD, *Interim Report of the Third Ad Hoc Group of Experts on Restrictive Business Practices to the Committee of Manufactures at Its Eighth Session* (Geneva, 1977).
15. Ibid., p. 12.
16. Ibid., pp. 12–15.
17. UNCTAD, *Report of the Intergovernmental Group of Experts on an International Code of Conduct on Transfer of Technology to the United Nations Conference on an International Code of Conduct on Transfer of Technology* (Geneva, July 1978), pp. 8–10.
18. OECD, *International Investment and Multinational Corporations* (Paris, 1976), pp. 11–12.
19. Ibid.
20. For example, the ILO is a specialized agency concerned with aspects of employment.
21. See ILO, *Tripartite Declaration of Principles concerning Multinational Enterprises and Social Policy* (Geneva, 1977).
22. Most studies on the employment aspects of transnationals tend to arrive at this conclusion. It is true that trends appeared to be changing somewhat over the years, largely as a result of government and trade union pressures.
23. ILO, *Tripartite Declaration*.

24. See S. K. Asante, "United Nations: International Regulation of Transnational Corporations," *Journal of World Trade Law* 13, no. 1 (1979):57.

25. Ibid., p. 56.

26. Ibid., pp. 59–61.

NAME INDEX

Aaronovitch, S., 11
Ames, E., 51
Amin, S., 27
Averch, H., 51

Baldwin, R., 25
Baran, P., 27
Bauer, P., 24
Baumol, W. J., 51
Beckford, G., 56, 82
Boeke, J., 22

Cairncross, A., 25
Caves, R., 53
Chamberlain, E. H., 3, 6, 7
Clark, J. M., 12
Cournot, A., 5–6
Cowling, K., 16

Downie, J., 12

Edwards, C., 53
Ekaus, R., 22

Fine, R., 78
Frank, A., 27

Galbraith, J. K., 11, 12, 15
Griffin, K., 29

Hall, R., 51
Harrod, R., 9
Hicks, J. R., 19
Higgins, B., 22
Hirschman, A., 24
Hitch, C., 51
Hunter, A., 11
Hymer, S., 54

Jewkes, J., 16
Johnson, L., 51

Kabunda, M. K., 83, 84
Kafoglis, M. J., 51
Kaldor, N., 15, 20
Kantzenbach, E., 12
Kindleberger, C., 25
Kipling, J., 16
Knickerbocker, E., 53

Lall, S., 56, 92, 114
Lever, W., 83
Lewis, W. A., 21, 22, 25, 26

McGuire, J. W., 51
Malthus, T., 20
Markham, J., 9
Meek, G., 16
Meller, R., 56
Mueller, D., 16
Mueller, W., 56
Myrdal, G., 24

Newfarmer, R., 56, 91

O'Brien, D., 16

Papandreou, A., 51
Penrose, E., 86
Pickering, J. F., 16

Reed, S. R., 16
Roberts, D. R., 51
Robinson, J., 3

Rostow, W., 23
Rowthorn, B., 54

Sawers, D., 16
Sawyer, M., 11
Schumpeter, J., 11, 15, 20, 21, 108
Scitovsky, T., 51
Simon, H., 10, 51
Singh, A., 16
Smith, A., 20
Sourrouille, J., 56
Sraffa, P., 3
Stackelberg, H. H. von, 7
Stigler, G. J., 9
Stillerman, R., 16
Streeten, P., 114
Sweezy, P. M., 10, 27

Tanzer, M., 86

Vaitsos, C., 52
Vernon, R., 52, 54, 81, 86, 87

White, E., 44
Whittington, G., 16
Williamson, O., 51
Willmore, L., 56
Wionczek, M., 26

Yamey, B., 24
Yip Hoong, 87

SUBJECT INDEX

Act against Restraints of Competition (1957), 34
Act against Unfair Competition (1909), 34
Act on Discounts and Rebates (1933), 34
Act on Penalties for Economic Offenses, 34
Africa: labor supplies in, 119; restrictive business practices in, 83–84
Agriculture, 20; transnational corporation activities in, 57–59, 61, 117, 119
Agriculture and Forestry Associations Act of 1962, 32
Aluminum industry, 87
Argentina, transnational exports of, 72
Automobile industry, 56, 60

Balance of payments, 114, 119–20
Banana industry, restrictive business practices in, 84–85

Banking, 56, 100
Bauxite, 87, 116
Booker McConnell, 57, 83
Boycotts, 76
Brand-name pooling, 7
Brazil: as exporter of technology, 128; restrictive business practices in electrical industry of, 90–91; transnational exports of, 72
Business Agreements Suspension Act, 37
Business concentration, 12–16; and corporate performance, 16; and transnational corporations, 56
Business firms, theories of operation, 2–3

Capital goods industry, restrictive business practices in, 91–92
Capital procurement, 114–15
Capper Volstead Act (1922), 32

Caribbean Community: export activities of, 117; industrial development in, 25–26; legislative control of restrictive business practices in, 42–43
Cartel activity, 15, 34, 35, 77, 88, 89, 99
Cartel Decree of 1941, 37
Clayton Act (1914), 30, 31
Climate, role of, in economic development, 24
Cocoa industry, restrictive business practices in, 85–86
Coconut cartel, 88
Collusiveness, 1–2, 5
Colombia: transfer pricing in, 97–98; transnational exports of, 72
Competition: dynamic approach to, 11–12; local vs. transnational, 109–10; monopolistic, 3; perfect, 2; stimulus to, by transnational corporations, 121
Concentration ratios, 12–13
Consumer protection, 34
Copper industry, restrictive business practices in, 86–87

Dependency, role of, in underdevelopment, 26
Developed countries, export structure of, 55
Developing countries: effects of transfer pricing on, 113; export promotion in, 60; exports of, 70–74; imports of, 65–70, 117; market structures in, 55–56; negative effects of transnational corporations on, 102–10; positive effects of transnational corporations on, 117, 118–21; transnational corporation activities in, 57–61
Development, theories of, 18–29
Division of labor, as key to productivity, 20
Dualism, 22

Economic Competition Act (1956), 37, 38
Economic Council of Mutual Aid (COMECON), 116

Economic development: defined, 18; "dependency school" of, 26; growth models for, 19; history of, 19–28; international integration in, 27–28; positive effects of transnational corporations on, 120; role of foreign aid in, 25–26; social scientific interpretation of, 28–29. *See also* Underdevelopment
Economic transformation, 120–21
Education, role of, in economic development, 24
Electrical industry, restrictive business practices in, 90–91
Employment, 104–05; impact on, by transnational corporations, 118–19
Engels Law, 22
Entrepreneur, role of, 20–21
Entrepreneurs' Agreements Act (1935), 37
Entropy, concept of, 52–53
Entry-forestalling strategies, 7, 9
European Economic Community (EEC), 14, 59, 116; legislative control of restrictive business practices within, 39–41
Export cartels, 15, 115
Export-Import Trading Act, 38
Exports: of developing countries by transnational corporations, 70–74; limitations of, 114, 115–16; promotion of, by transnational corporations, 118; restrictions on, 93–97

Fair Trading Act of 1973, 33, 34
Federal Republic of Germany: exports from developing countries to, 73; exports to developing countries by, 69; foreign direct investment by, 55, 63; legislative control of restrictive business practices in, 34–35; merger activity in, 13; statutory monopoly in, 3
Federal Trade Commission (FTC), 14, 32
Federal Trade Commission Act (1914), 30, 32

Finance Act (1963), 36
Foreign aid to developing countries,
    25–26
Foreign direct investment, 47, 49,
    51–52; breakdown of, by countries,
    62–65; and transnational corpora-
    tions, 55
France: foreign direct investment by, 63;
    legislative control of restrictive busi-
    ness practices in, 36–37; merger activ-
    ity in, 15; statutory monopoly in, 3

General Agreement on Tariffs and
    Trade (GATT), 124
General Foods, 88
Germany. See Federal Republic of
    Germany
Gini coefficient, 12–13
Growth, models of, 19
Guidelines for the Regulation of Acqui-
    sition of Assets, Mergers, and Take-
    overs (1974), 44

Havana Charter, 123, 124
Hong Kong, transnational exports
    from, 72

Imports: and balance of payments, 114;
    and capital procurement, 114–15; de-
    pendency of developing countries on,
    112–13; effects of transfer pricing on,
    113; pricing of, 111–12; and transna-
    tional corporations, 65–70
Income distribution, 28, 105–06
India: export restrictions in, 94–95; as
    exporter of technology, 128; legisla-
    tive control of restrictive business
    practices in, 43; transnational exports
    from, 72
Innovation, process of, 12
International Electrical Association, 90
International Labor Organization
    (ILO), 29, 99, 105, 106; work on
    restrictive business practices, 130
International production, 47, 48
Intracorporate loans, 45
Investment theory, 50–52, 53

Jamaica: as exporter of technology, 128;
    as plantation economy, 82
Japan: foreign direct investment by, 55;
    growth of transnational corporations
    in, 49–50; legislative control of re-
    strictive business practices in, 38–39;
    merger activity in, 15; transnational
    exports from, 69
Joint profit maximization, 7

Key Industries Control Act of 1931, 38
Kinked demand curve, 10

Labor supplies, role of, in economic
    growth, 20–21, 82–83. See also
    Employment
Latin America: export restrictions in,
    95–97; industrial growth in, 60; legis-
    lative control of restrictive business
    practices in, 44–46; transfer pricing
    in, 97–98; transnational exports from,
    72
Legislative control of restrictive business
    practices, 3, 30–46: in Caribbean
    Community, 42; in European Eco-
    nomic Community, 39–41; in Federal
    Republic of Germany, 34–35; in
    France, 36–37; in India, 43; in Japan,
    38–39; in Latin America, 44–46, in
    Malaysia, 44; in the Netherlands,
    37–38; in Pakistan, 43–44; in the
    United Kingdom, 32–34; in the United
    States, 30–32
Limit pricing, 4, 97
Lome Convention, 61, 107, 115
Lorenz curve, 12

McCarran Ferguson Act, 32
McGuire and Miller Tydings Act, 32
Malaysia: legislative control of restric-
    tive business practices in, 44; restric-
    tive business practices in tin industry
    of, 87–88
Manila Declaration (1976), 115
Manufacturing, transnational
    corporation activity in, 59–61

Marginal efficiency of capital (MEC), 50–51

Market domination, 2, 5; restrictive business practices as means to, 75–80

Market entry, freedom of, 2, 3

Market imperfection, models of, 2–11

Market sharing, 11

Mergers: growth of, 13–16; legislative control of, 33–34, 35; and transnational corporations, 53, 76

Mexico: export restrictions in, 95; as exporter of technology, 128; transnational exports from, 72–73

Mining: restrictive business practices in, 86–89; transnational corporation activity in, 57–59, 61

Molasses industry, restrictive business practices in, 88

Monopolies and Merger Act (1965), 33

Monopolies and Restrictive Business Practices Act of 1948, 32

Monopolies and Restrictive Business Practices Commission, 33

Monopolies and Restrictive Trade Practices Act of 1969, 43

Monopolies and Restrictive Trade Practices Ordinance, 43

Monopolistic competition, Chamberlain model of, 3

Monopoly: pure, 4–5; statutory, 3

Monopoly capitalism, 27

National Labor Relations Act, 32

Natural resource development, 103–04

Netherlands, legislative control of restrictive business practices in, 37–38

New International Economic Order, 103, 109, 115

Norris-La Guardia Act, 32

Obsolescence, forced, 113

Oil. See Petroleum industry

Oligopoly, 5–12; and conglomerate mergers, 15; leader-follower model of, 7–8; pricing behavior in, 8–11; and

transnational corporations, 54–55, 56

Oligopoly/duopoly, Cournot model of, 5–6

Organization for Economic Cooperation and Development (OECD): on collusion in capital goods industry, 91–92; on export cartels, 15, 115; on growth of mergers, 13, 15; work on restrictive business practices, 129–30

Output: growth of, 18–19; restrictions on, 104

Overpricing, 97, 98

Pakistan: legislative control of restrictive business practices in, 43–44; transnational exports from, 73

Patents, 35

Perfect competition, 2

Petroleum industry, 59, 86; foreign direct investment in, 61

Pharmaceutical industry, 92, 108

Philippines: export restrictions in, 93; restrictive business practices in, 92–93; transfer pricing in, 98

Plantation economies: restrictive business practices in, 82–86; and rural development, 102–03

Population growth, role of, in economic development, 20, 24

Price leadership, 8–10

Price rigidity, 111

Pricing, as a restrictive business practice, 2, 4, 7–10, 76, 77, 97–98, 107–09

Product allocation, as a restrictive business practice, 2, 76, 77, 99

Profits, and income distribution, 105–06

Quinine industry, restrictive business practices in, 89

Resale Prices Act of 1964, 32, 33

Resource misallocation, 5, 106–07

Restrictive business practices: collusiveness as, 1–2, 5; defined, 1; in employment, 104–05; and export restrictions,
93–97; impact of, on income distribution, 105–06; and import-substitution
activities, 90–91; limiting output, 104;
in mining, 86–89; negative impact of,
on developing countries, 102–10; in
plantation economies, 82–86; in price
fixing, 107–09; in resource allocation,
106–07; and rural development,
102–03; in technology transfer, 98,
110; in transfer pricing, 97–98, 113;
types of, 75–81; and work of
UNCTAD, 25, 27, 41, 72, 124–28
Restrictive Trade Practices Act of 1956,
32, 33
Restrictive Trade Practices Act of 1968,
33
Robinson-Patman Act (1936), 31
Rural development, 102–03

Saudi Arabia, 91
Sherman Act (1890), 30, 31
Singapore, transnational exports from,
73, 117
Southern Western Sugar and Molasses
Company, 88
Sweden, transnational exports from, 69
Switzerland, transnational exports
from, 69

Taiwan, transnational exports from, 73,
117
Tate and Lyle, 57, 82, 83
Tax evasion, 113
Technology acquisition, and restrictive
business practices, 78–81
Technology transfer: benefits of, to
developing countries, 119; domination of, by transnational corporations, 55; restrictions on, 98–99,
110
Tendering, collusion in, 91–92, 114–115
Tin industry, 87

Tourism, transnational corporation activity in, 61
Trade, theories of, 24–25
Trade Associations Act, 38
Transfer pricing, 45, 97–98, 113
Transformation curve, 18–19
Transnational corporations: and balance of payments, 114, 119–120; concentration of, in Latin America, 56;
and developing countries, 57–61; as
dominant-firm types, 52–57; and export cartels, 115; and exports of
developing countries, 70–74; growth
of, 49–50; and imports of developing
countries, 65–70; international production of, 47, 48; and intracorporate
pricing, 97; and investment theory,
51–52; mining activities of, 86–89;
negative impact of, on developing
countries, 102–10; and oligopolistic
markets, 54–55, 56; plantation activities of, 81–86; positive effects of, on
developing countries, 118–20; production activities of, by country, 62–65;
restrictive business activities of, in
nonprimary sector, 89–100 .
Treaty of Rome, 39–40

Underdevelopment, theories of, 21–29,
110
Underpricing, 97
Unemployment, 28
Unilever, 57, 82; restrictive business
practices by, 83–84
United Fruit Company (UFC), 82, 84, 85
United Kingdom: foreign direct investment by, 55, 63; legislative control of
restrictive business practices in,
32–34; merger activity in, 14; statutory monopoly in, 3; transnational exports from, 68
United Nations: Centre on Transnational Corporations, 130–32; Conference on Trade and Development
(UNCTAD), 25, 27, 41, 72, 124–28;

Conference on Trade and Employment, 123; and natural resource development, 103; study on market power,
99; study on transnational markets,
54
United States: foreign direct investment
by, 55, 63, 65; growth of transnational corporations in, 49-50; legislative control of restrictive business
practices in, 30-32; merger activity in,
13-14; statutory monopoly in, 3;
transnational corporation activities in
developing countries, 57-61, 66-68,
73

Webb-Pomerene Act (1918), 30, 32

Zaibatsus, 38, 39